U0929811

Key Concepts In Chinese Thought And Culture IX

中华思想文化术语

精装版

《中华思想文化术语》编委会 编

外语教学与研究出版社
FOREIGN LANGUAGE TEACHING AND RESEARCH PRESS
北京 BEIJING

图书在版编目（CIP）数据

中华思想文化术语. 第九辑 ：汉英对照 /《中华思想文化术语》编委会编. -- 北京 ：外语教学与研究出版社，2020.10
ISBN 978-7-5213-2152-4

Ⅰ. ①中… Ⅱ. ①中… Ⅲ. ①中华文化－术语－汉、英 Ⅳ. ①K203-61

中国版本图书馆 CIP 数据核字（2020）第 211936 号

出 版 人 徐建忠
责任编辑 刘 佳
责任校对 刘虹艳
装帧设计 奇文云海
出版发行 外语教学与研究出版社
社 址 北京市西三环北路 19 号（100089）
网 址 http://www.fltrp.com
印 刷 北京盛通印刷股份有限公司
开 本 710×1000 1/16
印 张 18.5
版 次 2020 年 11 月第 1 版 2020 年 11 月第 1 次印刷
书 号 ISBN 978-7-5213-2152-4
定 价 98.00 元

购书咨询：（010）88819926 电子邮箱：club@fltrp.com
外研书店：https://waiyants.tmall.com
凡印刷、装订质量问题，请联系我社印制部
联系电话：（010）61207896 电子邮箱：zhijian@fltrp.com
凡侵权、盗版书籍线索，请联系我社法律事务部
举报电话：（010）88817519 电子邮箱：banquan@fltrp.com
物料号：321520001

国家社会科学基金重大项目

“中华思想文化术语的整理、传播与数据库建设”（15ZDB003）

“十三五”国家重点出版物出版规划项目

获评第二届向全国推荐中华优秀传统文化普及图书

“中华思想文化术语传播工程”专家团队

（按音序）

Experts of the Key Concepts in Chinese Thought and Culture-Translation and Communication Project

顾问（Advisors）

李学勤（Li Xueqin）

林戊荪（Lin Wusun）

叶嘉莹（Florence Chia-ying Yeh）

张岂之（Zhang Qizhi）

专家委员会（Expert Board）

主任（Director）

韩　震（Han Zhen）

委员（Members）

晁福林（Chao Fulin）

陈德彰（Chen Dezhang）

陈明明（Chen Mingming）

冯志伟（Feng Zhiwei）

韩经太（Han Jingtai）

黄友义（Huang Youyi）

金元浦（Jin Yuanpu）

李建中（Li Jianzhong）

李照国（Li Zhaoguo）

楼宇烈（Lou Yulie）

马箭飞（Ma Jianfei）

聂长顺（Nie Changshun）

潘公凯（Pan Gongkai）

王　博（Wang Bo）

王　宁（Wang Ning）

叶　朗（Ye Lang）

袁济喜（Yuan Jixi）

袁行霈（Yuan Xingpei）

张立文（Zhang Liwen）

张西平（Zhang Xiping）

郑述谱（Zheng Shupu）

吕玉华（Lü Yuhua）
梅缵月（Mei Zuanyue）
裴德思（Thorsten Pattberg）
乔　永（Qiao Yong）
沈卫星（Shen Weixing）
孙艺风（Sun Yifeng）
童孝华（Tong Xiaohua）
王柯平（Wang Keping）
王　琳（Wang Lin）
王维东（Wang Weidong）
温海明（Wen Haiming）
吴志杰（Wu Zhijie）
徐亚男（Xu Yanan）
严文斌（Yan Wenbin）
杨雪冬（Yang Xuedong）
于文涛（Yu Wentao）
张建敏（Zhang Jianmin）
章思英（Zhang Siying）
赵　悠（Zhao You）
周云帆（Zhou Yunfan）
朱良志（Zhu Liangzhi）
左　励（Zuo Li）
满兴远（Man Xingyuan）
孟庆楠（Meng Qingnan）
乔　希（Joshua Mason）
任大援（Ren Dayuan）
施晓菁（Lynette Shi）
陶黎庆（Tao Liqing）
王刚毅（Wang Gangyi）
王丽丽（Wang Lili）
王明杰（Wang Mingjie）
魏玉山（Wei Yushan）
吴根友（Wu Genyou）
徐明强（Xu Mingqiang）
徐　英（Xu Ying）
严学军（Yan Xuejun）
杨义瑞（Yang Yirui）
余来明（Yu Laiming）
张　静（Zhang Jing）
赵　桐（Zhao Tong）
郑　开（Zheng Kai）
朱绩崧（Zhu Jisong）
朱　渊（Zhu Yuan）

前言

“中华思想文化术语”的定义可以表述为：由中华民族主体所创造或构建，凝聚、浓缩了中华哲学思想、人文精神、思维方式、价值观念，以词或短语形式固化的概念和文化核心词。它们是中华民族几千年来对自然与社会进行探索和理性思索的成果，积淀着中华民族的历史智慧，反映中华民族最深沉的精神追求以及理性思索的深度与广度；其所蕴含的人文思想、思维方式、价值观念已经作为一种“生命基因”深深融于中华子孙的血液，内化为中华民族共同的性格和信仰，并由此支撑起中华数千年的学术传统、思想文化和精神世界。它是当代中国人理解中国古代哲学思想、人文精神、思维方式、价值观念之变化乃至文学艺术、历史等各领域发展的核心关键，也是世界其他国家和民族了解当代中国、中华民族和海外华人之精神世界的钥匙。

当今世界已进入文化多元与话语多极时代。世界不同区域、不同国家、不同民族的文明，其流动融合之快、之广、之深超过历史任何时期。每个国家和民族都有自己独具的思想文化和话语体系，都应在世界文明、世界话语体系中占有一席之地，得到它应有的地位和尊重。而思想文化术语无疑是一个国家和民族话语体系中最核心、最本质的部分，是它的思想之“髓”、文化之“根”、精神之“魂”、学术之“核”。越来越多的有识之士认识到，中华思想文化蕴藏着解决当今人类所面临的许多难题的重要启示，中华民族所倡导的“厚德载物”“道法自然”“天人合一”“和而不同”“民惟邦本”“经世致用”等思想，以及它所追求的“协和万邦”“天下一家”、世界“大同”，代表了当今世界文明的发展趋势，也因此成为国际社会的共识。越来越多的外国学者和友人对中华思想文化及其术语产生浓厚的兴趣，希望有更全面、更进一步的了解。

今天我们整理、诠释、译写、传播中华思想文化术语，目的是立足于中华传统的思想文化，通过全面系统的整理与诠释，深度挖掘其中既能反映中华哲学思想、人文精神、思维方式、价值观念、文化特征，又具跨越时空、超越国度之意义，以及富有永恒魅力与当代价值的含义和内容，并将其译成英语等语言，让世界更客观、更全面地认识中国，了解中华民族的过去和现在，了解当代中国人及海外华人的精神世界，从而推动国家间的平等对话及不同文明间的交流借鉴。

中华思想文化术语的整理、诠释和英语译写得到了中国教育部、中国国际出版集团、中央编译局、北京大学、中国人民大学、武汉大学、北京外国语大学等单位的大力支持，得到了叶嘉莹、李学勤、张岂之、林戊荪等海内外众多知名学者的支持。需要说明的是，“中华思想文化术语”

这个概念是首次提出，其内涵和外延还有待学界更深入的研究；而且，如此大规模地整理、诠释、译写中华思想文化术语，在中国也是首次，无成例可循。因此，我们的诠释与译写一定还有待完善的地方，我们会及时吸纳广大读者的意见，不断提高术语诠释与译写的质量。

2015 年 4 月 11 日

FOREWORD

By "key concepts in Chinese thought and culture" we mean concepts and keywords or phrases the Chinese people have created or come to use and that are fundamentally pertinent to Chinese philosophy, humanistic spirit, way of thinking, and values. They represent the Chinese people's exploration of and rational thinking about nature and society over thousands of years. These concepts and expressions reflect the Chinese people's wisdom, their profound spiritual pursuit, as well as the depth and width of their thinking. Their way of thinking, values, and philosophy embodied in these concepts have become a kind of "life gene" in Chinese culture, and have long crystallized into the common personality and beliefs of the Chinese nation. For the Chinese people today, they serve as a key to a better understanding of the evolutions of their ancient philosophy, humanistic spirit, way of thinking, and values as well as the development of Chinese literature, art, and history. For people in other countries, these concepts open the door to understanding the spiritual world of contemporary China and the Chinese people, including those living overseas.

In the era of cultural diversity and multipolar discourse today, cultures of different countries and civilizations of different peoples are integrating faster, in greater depth, and on a greater scope than ever before. All countries and peoples have their own systems of thought, culture, and discourse, which should all have their place in the civilization and discourse systems of the world. They all deserve due respect. The concepts in thought and culture of a country and its people are naturally the most essential part of their discourse. They constitute the marrow of a nation's thought, the root of its culture, the soul of its spirit, and the core of its scholarship. More and more people of vision have come to recognize the inspirations Chinese thought and culture might offer to help resolve many difficult problems faced by mankind. The Chinese hold that a man should "have ample virtue and carry all things," "Dao operates naturally," "heaven and man are united as one," a man of virtue seeks "harmony but not uniformity," "people are the foundation of the state," and "study of ancient classics should meet present needs." The Chinese ideals such as "coexistence of all in harmony," "all the people under heaven are one family," and a world of "universal harmony" are drawing increasing attention among the international community. More and more international scholars and friends have become interested in learning and better understanding Chinese thought and culture in general, and the relevant concepts in particular.

In selecting, explaining, translating, and sharing concepts in Chinese thought and culture, we have adopted a comprehensive and systematic approach. Most of them not only reflect the characteristics of Chinese philosophy, humanistic spirit, way of thinking, values, and culture, but also have significance and/or implications that transcend time and national boundaries, and that still fascinate present-day readers and offer them food for thought. It is hoped that the translation of these concepts into English and other languages will help people in other countries to gain a more objective and more rounded understanding of China, of its people, of its past and present, and of the spiritual world of contemporary Chinese. Such understanding should be conducive to promoting equal dialogue between China and other countries and exchanges between different civilizations.

The selection, explanation, and translation of these concepts have been made possible thanks to the support of the Ministry of Education, China International Publishing Group, the Central Compilation and

Translation Bureau, Peking University, Renmin University of China, Wuhan University, and Beijing Foreign Studies University, as well as the support of renowned scholars in China and abroad, including Florence Chia-ying Yeh, Li Xueqin, Zhang Qizhi, and Lin Wusun.

The idea of compiling key concepts in Chinese thought and culture represents an innovation and the project calls much research and effort both in connotation and denotation. Furthermore, an endeavor like this has not been previously attempted on such a large scale. Lack of precedents means there must remain much room for improvement. Therefore, we welcome comments from all readers in the hope of better fulfilling this task.

April 11, 2015

目录
CONTENTS

哀吊

／āidiào／

Essay of Mourning and Essay of Memory

古代文体名称，用于哀悼死者或对遭遇不幸者表示慰问。“哀”的意思是哀悼、哀悯，最早用于哀悼夭折短寿的人，后也用于哀悯身遭不幸的人或不幸的事；“吊”的意思是凭吊，是对逝者表达追思或对遭遇不幸之事的人、国家等表示慰问。从哀吊对象说，“哀”一般用于当下的人或事，而“吊”常用于古人。从文体上说两者区别不大，略相当于今天的悼词，属于应用文，有些可以视为悼亡、怀古类的抒情散文。刘勰（465？—520）在《文心雕龙》中指出，哀辞重在表达对未及立德建功者的痛惜之情，因此不必追求辞藻；吊文多用于缅怀古人，因此常寓一定褒贬评价，具有反思和感怀的特点。这些见解对于今天的散文写作仍有指导意义。

Ai (哀) and *diao* (吊) essays were written in ancient times to express mourning for someone who had died a natural death or from an extreme misfortune. *Ai*, or an essay of mourning, was written to express grief or compassion. It was originally written for someone who died young; later, it was written to mourn a person's miserable life or unfortunate encounters. *Diao*, or an essay of memory, was intended to express one's deep affection for a long-deceased person or to offer his sincere condolences to the fatal misfortune suffered by a particular country or an individual. An essay of mourning was usually written for a recently deceased person, whereas an essay of memory showed one's abiding love for someone who died long ago. Stylistically, there is much resemblance between these two types of writing. They were like today's condolence speeches delivered at funerals, and some may be characterized as mourning or nostalgic lyrical essays. As Liu Xie (465?-520) put it in his literary critique *The Literary Mind and the Carving of Dragons*, *ai*, or an essay of mourning, expresses sorrow for the deceased person's yet unaccomplished merits, so it need not be excessively rhetorical in style. *Diao*, or an essay of memory, on the other hand, often shows one's love for someone who died long ago, so it may contain an evaluation of his life tinged with sentimental attachment. Liu's views still influence prose writing today.

引例 Citations:

◎奢体为辞，则虽丽不哀；必使情往会悲，文来引泣，乃其贵耳。（刘勰《文心雕龙·哀吊》）

（以浮夸文风写作哀辞，虽然华丽却不会使人哀伤；一定要让所抒之情出于内心悲痛，写出的文辞使人悲泣，这才是可贵的作品。）

Ai, an essay of mourning, written in a pompous style, beautiful as it may sound, will not really arouse a sense of grief among its readers. Only an essay which expresses one's deeply felt emotions and moves readers to tears can be regarded as a truly remarkable essay. (Liu Xie: *The Literary Mind and the Carving of Dragons*)

◎夫吊虽古义，而华辞未造；华过韵缓，则化而为赋。固宜正义以绳理，昭德而塞违，割析褒贬，哀而有正，则无夺伦矣。（刘勰《文心雕龙·哀吊》）

（“吊”的意义虽然很古，但写得华丽则是后来的事情；华丽过分而节奏弛缓，就演变为“赋”了。应该端正意义而斟酌事理，彰显美德而防范过失，辨析善恶而加以褒贬，表达哀情而内容纯正，这样就不会违背吊文的写作原则了。）

Although the meaning of *diao*, or an essay of memory can be traced a long way back, it was much later that an essay of memory became excessively rhetorical in style. If such an essay is written in a flowery style and drags on, it would look more like *fu* or rhapsodic prose. In writing an essay of memory, one should focus on a key message and explains its relevance, extol virtue and warn against errors, distinguish right from wrong and make evaluation accordingly, and express grief without distracting from the core message. These are rules to be observed in writing essays of memory. (Liu Xie: *The Literary Mind and the Carving of Dragons*)

爱类

/àilèi/

Love One's Own Kind

爱自己的同类，爱人类。中国古人认为，爱同类是有知觉或有灵性的动物的基本属性，作为万物灵长的人类亦然。人的爱心，首先表现在爱自己的同类上，生而为人，如果爱其他事物而不爱人类，就不能叫有爱心。也即是说，人是人类爱的第一对象，爱人类是人类爱的第一本质，也是人爱其他事物的精神原点。人之为人的基本规定性亦在于此。

The ancient Chinese considered loving others of one's own kind to be part of the fundamental nature of animals with consciousness and intelligence, and this was particularly true of humans, the most advanced of all creatures. Human love is first of all manifested in love for one's own kind. If a human loves other beings but not his or her fellow humans, that is not true love. Thus, human love first of all reaches other human beings, and love for humans is the fundamental nature of human love and also the origin of love for other creatures. So to love other human beings is a defining attribute of human beings.

引例 Citations:

◎凡生乎天地之间者，有血气之属必有知，有知之属莫不爱其类。……故有血气之属莫知于人，故人之于其亲也至死无穷。（《荀子·礼论》）

（凡是生于天地之间的人和物，只要有血气的就必然会有知觉，有知觉的没有不亲爱其同类的。……有血气的动物中，人最有灵性，所以人对自己父母的爱，到死也不会穷尽。）

All things born between heaven and earth with vital force have consciousness; and with consciousness they all love their own kind... Among those with vital force, none are more intelligent than humans; that is why humans have eternal love for their parents. (*Xunzi*)

◎仁于他物，不仁于人，不得为仁；不仁于他物，独仁于人，犹若为仁。仁也者，仁乎其类者也。故仁人之于民也，可以便之，无不行也。（《吕氏春秋·爱类》）

（对其他物类仁爱，对人却不仁爱，不能算有仁爱；对其他物类不仁爱，只对人仁爱，仍算有仁爱。所谓仁爱，是对自己的同类仁爱。所以，有仁德的治国者，只要是对百姓有利的事情，全都去做。）

If he loves other things but not his fellow human beings, he is not a man with true love. If he loves human beings but not other things, he is still a man with true love. The love we talk about is love for one's own kind. Therefore, a ruler with love who governs a country will do all the things beneficial to the people. (*Master Lü's Spring and Autumn Annals*)

◎遍知万物而不知人道，不可谓智；遍爱群生而不爱人类，不可谓仁。仁者爱其类也，智者不可惑也。（《淮南子·主术训》）

（遍识天下万物却不懂世态人情，不能称有智慧；遍爱天下生物却不爱人类，不能称有仁爱。所谓有仁爱，就是爱自己的同类；所谓有智慧，就是遇事不会疑惑。）

If he knows everything in the world, but not human feelings, he is not regarded as an intelligent man. If he loves all the living things in the world but not human beings, he is not regarded as a man with true love. The love that we talk about is to love one's own kind; the intelligence that we have in mind is the ability to see things for what they are. (*Huainanzi*)

爱人深者求贤急

/ài rén shēn zhě qiú xián jí/

Those Who Most Love the People Will Eagerly Seek Talent.

深爱民众的人，必然求贤心切。“贤”指德才出众的人，即优秀人才；“人”这里指民众，“爱人”即“爱民”。这里所说的“爱”，不是一般意义上的私德或个人关怀，而是指执政者把国家治理好，以保障人民的基本福祉和根本利益，使人民免受痛苦和无端侵害，安居乐业。而要达此目标，必须依靠德才出众的人来治理国家。所以，真心深爱民众的执政者，必然求贤若渴。“爱人”是根本，“求贤”是具体措施。

Someone who deeply cares about the people will have a strong desire to seek out talent. “Talent” refers to outstanding people, namely those with high morals and skills; “the people” refers to the general public, and “loving the people” means “caring about the people.” The term “love” as used here does not refer to personal morality or individual affection; it refers to how administrators must govern a country well so as to ensure the basic well-being and interests of its people, to spare them from suffering and unwarranted infringements, and to enable them to live stably and work happily. To achieve this, administrators must rely on outstanding people for the country's governance; hence administrators who truly care about the people will of course have a strong desire to find talent. “To love the people” is fundamental, and “to seek talent” is its specific means of implementation.

引例 Citation:

◎爱人深者求贤急，乐得贤者养人厚。(《素书·安礼》)

（深爱民众的人，必然求贤心切；得到贤才就喜悦的人，必然待人优厚。）

Someone who cares deeply about the people will eagerly seek out talent; someone who rejoices in finding talent will treat them well. (Huangshigong's Strategies on White Silk)

兵贵胜，不贵久

/bīng guì shèng, bù guì jiǔ/

In War, Seek Quick Victory, Not Prolongation.

用兵贵在速胜，不宜持久。这是古代军事家孙武提出的作战原则。对于主动作战的一方而言，这一原则尤为重要。因为久战不决，会造成士气低落、战斗力下降，各种消耗增大，补给困难，最终难以达成作战目标，甚至得不偿失，还可能节外生枝，危及国家安全。这是综合政治、经济等多种因素而形成的总体战争思想。

Warfare should seek a quick victory and should not be prolonged. This was a principle of warfare proposed by Sunzi, the ancient military strategist. It is of particular importance to the party that initiates a war. If the war continues without a decisive outcome, it will result in poor morale, weakened combat ability, an increase in various types of consumption, and difficulty in maintaining supply lines. Ultimately it will be hard to achieve the aims of the war and losses may even exceed gains; complications may also ensue which endanger the country's security. This is a comprehensive concept of war which incorporates political, economic and other factors.

引例 Citation:

◎其用战也胜，久则钝兵挫锐，攻城则力屈（jué），久暴师则国用不

足。……故兵贵胜，不贵久。故知兵之将，民之司命，国家安危之主也。（《孙子·作战篇》）

（用兵的关键是制胜，一旦持久作战就会造成军队疲惫、锐气受挫，攻城则兵力无法施展，长期陈兵在外，国家费用就会出现困难。……所以用兵贵在速胜，不宜持久。因此可以说，精通兵法的将帅，是掌握民众命运、决定国家安危的关键人物。）

The crux of war is gaining a victory. Hence prolonged warfare tires the troops and saps their morale; they will be thwarted when attacking cities; if they are deployed away from home for a long time, the country's finances will be in difficulty... Hence warfare should seek quick victory and not prolongation. Thus a commander who is skilled in warfare controls the destiny of his people and is master of his country's security. (*The Art of War*)

不二

/bù'èr/

Advaya / Non-duality

离两边。指超越一切分别，对一切现象都平等如一。凡夫通常以二分的模式理解世间现象，说常、无常，得、无得。佛教认为，二分法构建出一幅虚妄分别的世界图景，并不能如实反映世界的真实情况。而任何建立在言语概念基础上的认识，都无法避免这种分别。因此要离开两边，摆脱名言的误导，从而远离凡夫的分别，到达平等如一的空性智慧。

The concept of *advaya* instructs one to avoid the two extremes, to transcend all distinctions, and to treat all phenomena equally. A common man often understands the world in dichotomy, creating a number of opposites such as permanence versus impermanence and possession versus dispossession. Buddhists believe that dichotomy paints the picture of a world full of fantasies and distinctions, failing to truthfully reflect the reality. Such fantasies and distinctions are automatic in any understanding based on verbal concepts. Therefore, one shall avoid the two extremes and the misleading of worldly names and words. In this way can one transcend the distinctions perceived by a common man and achieve the ultimate wisdom of equality and emptiness.

引例 Citation:

◎于一切法无言无说，无示无识，离诸问答，是为入不二法门。

(《维摩诘所说经·入不二法门品》)

(对于所有事物无所言说，无所指示，也无所认识，远离各种问答判断，才可谓进入不二的境界。)

If one has no word about, comment on, reference to, or even knowledge of anything and stays away from questions, answers, or judgment concerning anything, one can arrive at the state of *advaya* through the dharma gate. (*The Teaching of Vimalakīrti*)

苍生大医

/cāngshēng-dàyī/

A Master Physician to All the People

众生景仰的伟大医者，百姓的好医生。这是唐朝著名医学家孙思邈(581-682) 在《千金方》中所阐述的理想的医者形象。“苍生”即众生，主要指百姓；“大医”即超乎寻常的、伟大的、令人尊敬的医者。这样的医者有三种基本品格或精神：一是平等，不论患者贫富贵贱、亲疏善恶、同族异族，均一视同仁；二是仁爱，视患者为亲人，悲悯至深，感同身受；三是无私，将个人安危、利益置之度外，一心治病救人。它是“大医精诚”理念的重要组成部分，是“医者仁心”这一中华医学人道精神的最高体现。

This term means a great physician held in high esteem by everyone, a good doctor for all the people. This is the ideal image of a physician as described by the famous Tang Dynasty physician Sun Simiao (581-682) in his *Essential Formulas for Emergencies*. “All the people” refers mainly to the general populace; a “master physician” is an extraordinary doctor who is great and commands respect. Such a doctor has three basic qualities or spirits: the first is equality, treating all patients with the same care regardless of wealth, social status, or kinship ties; the second is caring, treating all patients as kin, with the deepest compassion and empathy; the third is selflessness, focusing only on treating patients without regard for personal safety or personal interests. This is the most important component of the concept that “a master physician must have superb skill and sincerity," and the highest manifestation of "the caring heart of a physician," which is the humanist spirit of Chinese medicine.

引例 Citation:

◎若有疾厄来求救者，不得问其贵贱贫富，长幼妍媸（chī），怨亲善友，华夷愚智，普同一等，皆如至亲之想。亦不得瞻前顾后，自虑吉凶，护惜身命，见彼苦恼，若己有之，深心凄怆，勿避险巇（xī），昼夜寒暑，饥渴疲劳，一心赴救，无作工夫形迹之心。如此可为苍生大医，反此则是含灵巨贼。（孙思邈《千金方·论大医精诚》）

（如果有疾病苦痛来求医者，则不论其身份贵贱、家中贫富、年纪长幼、长相美丑、品行善恶，是亲友还是怨仇，是汉族还是异族以及智力高下，均一视同仁，就像对待自己至亲一样。也不能瞻前顾后，考虑个人的安危得失，爱惜自己的身家性命，而要把病人的苦痛当成自己的痛苦，深怀悲悯之心，不避路途险阻，不管昼夜寒暑，不怕饥渴疲劳，一心只想着救助病人，不要费工夫想着如何沽名钓誉。这样才能成为天下苍生尊崇的医者，反之则是众生的巨大祸害。）

All patients seeing a doctor should be treated equally like family, regardless of their social status, wealth, age, physical appearance, or conduct, regardless of whether they are friends or enemies, whether they are Han or other ethnic groups, whether they are intelligent or not. The doctor must not be worrying right and left, considering personal gains or risks, or caring more about his own property, family or safety of life; he must treat the patient's suffering as his own, be filled with compassion, fear no obstacles, disregard day and night, heat and cold, hunger and thirst, and think only of helping the sick. He must not be thinking of his fame or reputation. Only in this way can he become a master physician to all the people; otherwise he will bring disaster to everyone. (Sun Simiao: *Essential Formulas for Emergencies*)

称情立文

/chēngqíng-lìwén/

Establish Moral Standards in Keeping with Human Feelings

依据情感而制定礼的规范。称：权衡。出自《礼记》和《荀子》。儒家认识到，人的情感是自然生发的，需要获得适当的抒发与表达。这种情感诉求也对人的言行乃至人伦秩序有着不可回避的影响。要实现有序而稳定的人伦生活，需要对个体的情感做出适当的安顿，而不是一味地加以抑制。因此，礼对于人伦生活的规范，要以情感的合理诉求为依据。

This concept originated in *The Book of Rites* and *Xunzi*. The Confucian view is that human emotions arise naturally and need to be properly expressed. They have an inescapable influence on people's conduct and their moral behavior. To maintain an orderly and stable moral order, it is important that the emotions of people are properly expressed and not indiscriminately suppressed. Therefore, moral standards should be based on people's reasonable desire.

引例 Citation:

◎三年之丧，何也？曰：称情而立文，因以饰群，别亲疏贵贱之节，而弗可损益也。（《礼记·三年问》）

（三年之丧是根据什么而定的呢？回答道：依据人的哀戚之情而订立的礼仪，由此来规范人伦的秩序，区别人与人之间亲疏贵贱的关系，是不可以随便减损或增益的。）

Why should the mourning period for one's parents last for three years? The answer is that it is based on the degree of the mourner's grief. Such a rule, which determines the order of human relations and differentiates the closeness between people and their social positions, should not be altered by cutting it short or extending it longer at will. (*The Book of Rites*)

耻

/chǐ/

Shame

羞耻，是一种重要的道德心理。在人们认同于某种道德的前提下，一旦发现自身的言行背离了道德的规范，就会自觉地产生愧疚、自责的心理，这即是所谓的“耻”。儒家将这种道德心理的建立，视为人伦教化的重要目标。儒家不只要求人们遵守外在的道德规范，还要求人们对于道德行为有着发自于内的认同，通过羞耻之心实现自我的道德约束。“耻”后来也用作对不道德言行的一种评价，即“可耻”。

Shame is an important part of moral psychology. Once there are commonly accepted morals and once people find that their own words and deeds violate those morals, they will consciously feel guilt and self-reproach – this is known as “shame.” Confucians considered the development of such a moral psychology to be an important goal of ethics education. In addition to wanting people to abide by external moral norms, they also wanted them to develop an internal awareness of moral behavior, and to achieve moral self-constraint through a sense of shame. This term was later used to judge immoral words and deeds, i.e., shameful.

引例 Citations:

◎子贡问曰：“何如斯可谓之士矣？”子曰：“行己有耻，使于四方，

不辱君命，可谓士矣。”（《论语·子路》）

（子贡请教：“如何做才可以称为士？”孔子说：“对自己的言行保持羞耻之心，出使四方诸侯，不辱没君主赋予的使命，就可以称为士了。”）

Zigong asked, “What qualifies a person to be called a *shi* (roughly referring to those at the social stratum between the aristocracy and the common people)?” Confucius said, “He who conducts himself with a sense of shame, and does not disgrace the tasks entrusted by his sovereign when dispatched elsewhere, may be called a *shi*.” (*The Analects*)

◎子曰：“道之以政，齐之以刑，民免而无耻。道之以德，齐之以礼，有耻且格。”（《论语·为政》）

（孔子说：“用政令加以引导，用刑罚加以规范，民众能免于罪过，但没有羞耻之心。用道德加以引导，用礼义加以规范，民众不但有羞耻之心，而且能够自觉合于规范。”）

Confucius said, “If people are guided by governmental decree and made to behave themselves through punishments, they will avoid punishment, but will have no sense of shame. If they are guided by morality and behave themselves in accordance with social norms, they will have a sense of shame and will follow rules.” (*The Analects*)

赤子之心

／chìzǐzhīxīn／

Utter Innocence

本义指婴儿未经世俗染污的纯洁心灵，也指成年人仍然保有的婴儿般的赤诚真心，那种在功利世界里仍能坚守的初心。在政治伦理领域，它指人类善良的真心本性，主要是推己及人的恻隐之心或者是童真一般的尚实求真的品格；在文艺创作与审美领域，它主要指具有丰富情感和美好纯真理想的童心，是超越了一切功利心、尘俗气息以及过于理智、缺乏审美情趣的心理状态。它既是古人推崇的理想人格的一种表征，也是文艺作品中美好人物形象塑造的一种类型。

This term refers to the pure heart and soul of a newborn babe, untainted by worldly affairs. Most often, it refers to adults who retain the utter innocence of an infant, holding themselves aloof from worldly goals. In the field of political ethics, the term highlights humans' natural kindness, calling for empathy with others and child-like wonder for truth. In literary creation and aesthetics, it refers mainly to a pure state of being filled with subtle feelings and noble ideals, transcending all worldly pursuits and sophistication, and rejecting an overly rational mentality lacking aesthetic judgment. The term promotes an ideal personality worshiped by ancient Chinese and represents a laudable type of character often portrayed in literary works.

引例 Citations:

◎含德之厚，比于赤子。蜂虿（chài）虺（huǐ）蛇不螫（shì），猛兽不据，攫鸟不搏。骨弱筋柔而握固，未知牝牡之合而全作，精之至也。终日号而不嗄，和之至也。知和曰常，知常曰明，益生曰祥，心使气曰强。物壮则老，谓之不道，不道早已。（《老子·五十五章》）

（含有深厚德性的人，比得上初生的婴儿。有毒的虫蛇不会叮咬他，猛兽不会伤害他，凶禽不会捕捉他。他筋骨柔弱但拳头握得很紧，不知道男女交合但生殖器却能勃起，这是因为精气充足的缘故。他整天号哭但是嗓子不沙哑，这是因为元气醇和的缘故。理解醇和的道理，就懂得了恒常，懂得了恒常，就可称为明智。纵欲贪生会有不祥，精气任由欲望支配就是逞强。事物过于强盛就会衰老，这叫不合自然常道，不合自然常道就会很早衰亡。）

A man of profound virtue is like a newborn babe. Venomous insects will not sting him, snakes will not bite him, beasts will not harm him, and ferocious birds will not prey on him. He is by no means strong physically, but keeps his fists tightly clenched. Although he knows nothing about intercourse with a woman, his genital hardens because he is full of vital energy. He wails all day without getting hoarse because his energy is mellow. An appreciation of mellow energy promises an understanding of permanence. This, in turn, is akin to wisdom. Indulging in sensual pleasures and unscrupulously craving for life will incur misfortune. If vital energy is dictated by desire, that is an outrageous flaunt. Excessive strength marks the beginning of aging, for it goes against the way of nature. Any violation of this rule will lead to one's fall. (*Laozi*)

◎大人者，不失其赤子之心者也。（《孟子·离娄下》）

（有德行的人，是能保持婴儿般天真纯朴之心的人。）

He who is capable of retaining a childlike heart is a truly virtuous man. (*Mencius*)

冲淡

／chōngdàn／

Quiet Elegance

冲和平淡。用于文艺批评，主要指语言平和质朴、意境闲适恬静的一种诗歌风格。它看似空无所有，实则充盈无限；看似平淡无奇，实则意味悠长。这多与作者冲和平淡的性情相应，反映作者尝遍人生百味之后的心态与境界，是超越一切语言表达与文章法则的真情流露。冲淡作为一种美学理念，不仅影响到文艺创作，也塑造文人学士的心性，影响他们的人生态度。

This term is used in literary criticism to refer to a poetic style marked by the plainness and simplicity of wording and by a leisurely quietude. Despite its seeming sterility, such a style is full of life's potentialities and possesses a profound appeal. This echoes the author's mild and placid temperament, showing his mental attitude and spiritual realm of life after he has gone through life's hardships and struggles – a natural expression of feeling which transcends all forms of verbal articulation and all rules of writing. As an aesthetic notion, quiet elegance has not only influenced artistic creation but also shaped the spiritual being of men of letters, helping to cultivate their outlook on life.

引例 Citations:

◎以虚诞而为高古，以缓慢而为冲淡。（释皎然《诗式·诗有六迷》）

（把虚妄荒诞当作高远古朴，把节奏松缓当作冲和平淡。）

Fabrication and absurdity are mistaken for loftiness and primitive simplicity, and languidness for quiet elegance. (Shi Jiaoran: *Poetic Styles*)

◎唐初王、杨、沈、宋擅名，然不脱齐梁之体。独陈拾遗首倡高雅冲澹之音，一扫六代之纤弱，趋于黄初、建安矣。（刘克庄《后村诗话》卷一）

（唐朝初年，只有王勃、杨炯、沈佺期、宋之问享有盛名，但是尚未摆脱齐梁时期追求形式绮丽的风格。唯独陈子昂最先发出诗歌应当高雅冲淡的声音，一扫六朝以来的纤细柔弱，写作风格自此开始向黄初、建安时期的诗歌靠拢。）

In the early Tang period, Wang Bo, Yang Jiong, Shen Quanqi, and Song Zhiwen were the only ones who enjoyed widespread renown, yet none of them had freed themselves of the obsession with formal beauty pursued by poets of the Qi-Liang era. Chen Zi'ang alone argued for quiet elegance in poetry, making a clean sweep of the cloying sentimentality of the Six Dynasties. After that, the style of poetry shifted toward that of the Huangchu and Jian'an eras of the Wei Kingdom. (Liu Kezhuang: *Houcun's Poetic Remarks*)

◎陶渊明诗所不可及者，冲澹深粹，出于自然。（杨时《龟山集·语录·荆州所闻》）

（陶渊明的诗之所以为后人所不能及，是因为他的诗冲和平淡、深刻纯粹，完全出于自然性情的流露。）

Tao Yuanming's poetry has remained unrivaled because of its quiet elegance, profundity and purity. It fully shows his natural feelings. (Yang Shi: *Collected Essays of Yang Shi*)

词话

/cíhuà/

Criticism on *Ci* Poetry / *Cihua* (Story-telling with Song and Speech)

主要含义有二：其一，指评论词人、词作、词派，记述词的本事及相关考订的著作，是中国古代诗学文献的一个组成部分。词话借鉴诗话而来，滥觞于北宋，成熟于南宋。著名的词话著作有清代陈廷焯（1853—1892）的《白雨斋词话》、王国维（1877—1927）的《人间词话》等。《人间词话》是王国维在接受了西方美学理论之后，融汇中西美学思想，以崭新的眼光对中国词人与词作做出的评论。表面上看，《人间词话》沿袭了中国传统的诗话、词话一类作品的体例，实际上它已初具理论体系，是晚清以来最有影响的文艺批评著作之一。其二，指盛行于元、明两代的一种说唱艺术形式（其中的“词”主要指词曲），如《大唐秦王词话》，有说有唱，韵文、散文并用。由宋代说话伎艺发展而来，明代中叶以后，逐渐演变为弹词和鼓词两个系统，并且取代了“词话”名称。又，明后期及清前期“词话”还曾用来指称夹杂词曲的章回体通俗小说，如《金瓶梅词话》等。

This term has a two-fold meaning. First, it refers to any work that offers commentaries on *ci* poets, poems, schools of *ci* poetry, the gist of a *ci* poem and textual criticisms. This type of work is a constituent part of scholarly inquiry into classical Chinese poetry. Criticism on *ci* poetry, with relatively long lines interspersed with shorter ones, are derived from criticism on the more usual type of classical Chinese poetry with a fixed number of characters to a line. They proliferated in the Northern Song Dynasty and matured in the Southern Song Dynasty. Famed works of *ci* poetry appreciation include *Remarks on Ci Poetry from White Rain Studio* by Chen Tingzhuo (1853-1892) and *Poetic Remarks in the Human World* by Wang Guowei (1877-1927), both from the Qing Dynasty. The latter work, written after Wang Guowei was influenced by Western aesthetic theories, and fusing Chinese and Western aesthetic thoughts together, was a criticism work on Chinese *ci* poets and *ci* poems made from a brand-new perspective. Although superficially it imitates the traditional way of offering commentaries on *shi* poetry and *ci* poetry, it in fact already attempts to construct a theoretic system. It has remained the most influential work of literary criticism since the late-Qing period.

Second, the term *cihua* also refers to an art of theatrical performance combining narratives and songs popular in the Yuan and Ming dynasties, in which the *ci* part is the singing of rhymed verse. As in *Tales of Prince Qin of the Great Tang Dynasty*, the performance intersperses singing with narrative, and verse with prose. It was developed from the performance of story-telling with speech and song of the Song Dynasty. After the mid-Ming Dynasty, such performances started to adopt two new terms: *tanci* (弹词), or story-telling with the accompaniment of musical instruments such as the Chinese lute, and *guci* (鼓词), or story-telling aided by a drum and clapper. Still later, these two new terms superseded the old. From the last years of the Ming to the first years of the Qing, this term was sometimes also used to refer to a popular novel with each chapter headed by a couplet giving the gist of its content which was interspersed with beautiful verse, for example *Tales of the Golden Lotus*.

引例 Citations:

◎玩月新诗偏有趣，兴唐词话更消闲。（《大唐秦王词话》第四十六回）

（赏月的新诗实在有趣，但讲唱大唐兴起的词话更能使听众消闲。）

The new-style poetry in praise of the moon may be fun, but spoken and sung tales of Li Shimin's rise to the throne are far more intriguing. (*Tales of Prince Qin of the Great Tang Dynasty*)

◎词话者，纪词林之故实，辨词体之流变，道词家之短长也。（谢之勃《论词话》，《国专季刊》第一期）

（词话，用来记录词林的典故，辨析词体的流变，评论词家的优缺点。）

Commentaries on *ci* poetry record the classics of lyrical poetry, analyze the various styles of *ci* poetry, and enumerate the merits and shortcomings of *ci* poets. (Xie Zhibo: On *Ci* Poetry Commentaries)

但见性情，不睹文字

/dàn jiàn xìngqíng, bù dǔ wénzì/

To Impress Readers with True Feelings Oblivious of Its Wording

文学作品完美呈现作者的本性真情，让读者全身心感受到性情的真与美，而感觉不到文字的存在。由唐代诗僧皎然（720—796？）提出。此语一是强调性情为本，文字只是工具；二是强调写作者与接受者都要得意忘言；三是突出文学艺术以心会心的特点，只有通过心灵对话才能激活言语之外的多重意蕴。它体现了中国古代文学重视意象、意境构造的特点。

This happens when a literary work reveals to its reader the truth and beauty of its author's innermost feelings, to the point that the reader becomes oblivious to the wording. Such an idea was first raised by the Tang Dynasty poet-monk Jiaoran (720-796?). It emphasizes three points. First, the core value of literature is to express one's true feeling; the wording is only a tool. Second, both the author and reader should focus on the meaning while forgetting the words. Third, tacit understanding is crucial to art and literature. Only through dialogue between souls can a variety of illocutionary implications be activated. The whole term highlights the importance of imagery and artistic ambience in classical Chinese literature.

引例 Citations:

◎两重意已上，皆文外之旨，若遇高手如康乐公，览而察之，但见

情性，不睹文字，盖诣道之极也。（释皎然《诗式·重意诗例》）

（诗句具有两重以上的意蕴，都属于言外之旨。如果碰到谢灵运这样的高人，仔细阅读他的作品，你只会感受到诗人的本真性情，不会注意他的文字，这大概是因为他的作品已经臻至诗歌创作的最高境界了。）

Poetic lines carry two or more implications, lying outside of language itself. If you encounter a truly great poet such as Xie Lingyun, you will be struck with his bold and uninhibited expression of feeling and forget his wording. This is probably because his works have reached the highest level of poetic excellence. (Shi Jiaoran: *Poetic Styles*)

◎［杜甫《九日蓝田崔氏庄》］通首八句，一气夷犹，开合顿宕而出。但见情性，不睹文字。（方东树《昭昧詹言·续卷四·杜公》）

（通篇八句诗，好像有一股气从容行于其中，左右开合，跌宕起伏，直至完全抒泄。通篇只感受到诗人的本真情性，不会注意他的文字。）

This eight-line poem is permeated with a calmly executed vital energy. It is sometimes vigorous, sometimes quiet and elegant. It rises and falls rhythmically until it has given full vent to the author's pent-up feelings. So impressed with the author's true feelings, readers will pay no heed to his actual wording. (Fang Dongshu: *Rambling Words to Expose the Secrets of Poetry Writing*)

道不同，不相为谋

／dào bù tóng, bù xiāng wéi móu／

Part Ways and Part Company

走的路不同，不会在一起商量怎么走；人的主张、信念等不同，不会选择一道合作共事。“道”本指道路，这里泛指主张、信念、志趣、看法、行事原则等；“谋”本指谋划，引申指合作共事。对于合作共事而言，最重要的是彼此达成共同的目标原则，没有共同的目标原则，双方不可能顺利合作，但是也不能为了合作而放弃原则。坚持原则，不是拒绝合作，而是拒绝无原则的迁就。人与人共事，国与国合作，皆循此理。

Travelers heading down different paths do not plan together how to travel. Originally, the saying meant people with different views and beliefs do not seek to work together. *Dao* (道 way), which originally referred to "road," is extended to include opinions, beliefs, interests, viewpoints, and guiding principles. *Mou* (谋 plan), is extended to mean cooperation and collaboration. In order to work together, it is most important to agree upon a set of common goals and principles. Without them, parties cannot collaborate successfully. On the other hand, collaboration should not sacrifice principles. Upholding principles does not mean rejecting cooperation. Rather, it means rejecting unprincipled deal-making. This is true of cooperation among individuals and among countries as well.

引例 Citations:

◎子曰："道不同，不相为谋。"亦各从其志也。（《史记·伯夷列传》）

（孔子说："主张不同，不在一起谋事。"也就是各按自己的意愿行事。）

Confucius said, "People who differ in their principles do not work together." That is to say, they follow their own will in their action. (*Records of the Historian*)

◎友者，所以相有也。道不同，何以相有也？（《荀子·大略》）

（所谓朋友，就是相互拥有。双方的原则不同，用什么相互拥有呢？）

Friends are those who have commonalities. If they differ in principle, what can they share? (*Xunzi*)

道心

/dàoxīn/

Moral Mind / Moral Consciousness

符合道德原则的知觉意识。"道心"与"人心"对举，见于古文《尚书》、《荀子》等典籍。宋儒特别重视"道心"与"人心"的概念，对其含义进行了解释和发挥。宋儒认为，心的知觉活动包含两类内容：其一，依循于道德原则的知觉意识，即是"道心"。其二，由耳目等身体官能所生发的对外物的欲求，称为"人心"。"道心"源自天命所授的本性，合于天理，但往往隐微而不易显现。人应努力发挥"道心"的功用，以克服"人心"中过度的欲望。

The "moral mind" refers to people's awareness of moral principles. It is set in contrast to the "human heart," and appears in classics such as the "Old Text" version of *The Book of History*, and *Xunzi*. Confucian scholars in the Song Dynasty attached great importance to both terms and made interpretations and expositions about them. They believed that the conscious mind, or heart involved two aspects: one, conscious of moral principles, was *daoxin*, or the "moral mind"; the other, consumed with human desires aroused by the sensory organs such as eyes and ears, was called *renxin*, or the "human heart." The consciousness of moral principles in the "moral mind" comes from innate human nature working in agreement with heavenly principles, but it is elusive.

It needs to be allowed full play so that the excessive desires of the "human heart" can be held in check.

引例 Citations:

◎人心惟危，道心惟微，惟精惟一，允执厥中。(《尚书·大禹谟》)

（人心危险，道心隐微，用心应精审专一，诚实秉持中正之道。）

The human heart is beset by danger, while the moral mind is subtle and elusive. Concentration of mind is required for sticking to the path of justice and uprightness. (*The Book of History*)

◎心之虚灵知觉，一而已矣。而以为有人心、道心之异者，则以其或生于形气之私，或原于性命之正，而所以为知觉者不同，是以或危殆而不安，或微妙而难见（xiàn）耳。（朱熹《中庸章句序》）

（心的知觉意识，其实是同一个东西罢了。但"人心"和"道心"被认为有分别，是由于"人心"源自形体所禀受之气带来的私欲，"道心"源自天命之性中的正理，因此认为两种知觉有所不同，"人心"危险而不安定，"道心"隐微而不轻易显现。）

Consciousness and senses from the heart are ultimately the same thing. A distinction, however, may be made between the "human heart" and the "moral mind." This is because the former refers to selfish desires brought about by the bodily senses, whereas the latter comes from heavenly principles of justice. Human desires are dangerous and lead to uncertainty. Consciousness of moral principles is elusive and rarely exhibits itself. (Zhu Xi: Preface to *Annotations on The Doctrine of the Mean*)

德性

／déxìng／

Virtuous Nature / Morals as Human Nature

人的道德本性。最早见于《礼记·中庸》。古人普遍承认，人天生所具的本性之中包含着人对于外物的感知与欲求。但是，对于人性之中是否包含道德性的因素，古人则持有不同的见解。大部分儒者认为，人性之中同时还包含着仁义礼智等道德的根基，也即是"德性"。"德性"需要经过一定的修养工夫，才能最终成就善行。

This refers to people's innate moral nature. The term first appeared in *The Book of Rites*. Ancient Chinese people widely believed that inborn human nature had feelings and a craving for knowledge of the outside world. However, they had different views as to whether morals were included in innate human nature. The majority of Confucian scholars held that human nature had in itself a basic sense of benevolence, righteousness, rites and wisdom, and together they constituted the virtuous nature. Still these scholars maintained that self-cultivation was required for such nature to develop into conscious benevolence.

引例 Citations:

◎故君子尊德性而道问学，致广大而尽精微，极高明而道中庸。（《礼记·中庸》）

（因此君子尊崇德性又从事对知识学问的追求，使自己的认识广博又能极尽其精微之处，极为高明又能遵行中庸之道。）

Therefore, a man of integrity should revere the virtuous nature of human beings and constantly pursue knowledge. This way, he will acquire extensive knowledge and gain command of it in an in-depth way. He can thus reach mastery and observe the doctrine of the mean. (*The Book of Rites*)

◎德性者，非耳目口体之性，乃仁义礼智之根心而具足者也。（王夫之《张子正蒙注》卷二上）

（德性并不是耳、目、口、身体等官能的本性，而是仁义礼智根源、具备于心的本性。）

The virtuous nature is not that of ears, eyes, mouth and body, rather it is the source from which benevolence, justice, rites, and wisdom emerge. They actually come forth from one's heart. (Wang Fuzhi: *Annotations to Zhang Zai's Enlightenment Through Confucian Teachings*)

独抒性灵，不拘格套

／dú shū xìnglíng, bù jū gétào／

Bold Expression of One's True Self

文学创作抒发自己真实独特的性情，不拘泥于任何格式套路。原为明代文学家袁宏道（1568—1610）对其弟弟袁中道（1570—1626）文学创作的评语，后来成为公安派的核心理论主张，与当时前、后七子“文必秦汉，诗必盛唐”的复古主义观点形成了鲜明的对抗。公安派强调文艺源于个人性情，讲求独创性，重自由，反拘束，要求诗人不为成法所限。在当时尊古、模拟盛行的风气下，这一命题有个性解放和反传统的意义，对于当时及后代的文艺创作产生了积极影响。

This term indicates that a writer should give expression to his true feelings in literary creation and not be constrained by particular regulations or formulas. It was first used by the Ming Dynasty writer Yuan Hongdao (1568-1610) as he commented on the literary work of his younger brother Yuan Zhongdao (1570-1626). Later, it became the core idea of the Gong'an School of Literary Writing, firmly opposed to the stubborn emulation of ancient literature as advocated by the Former Seven Masters and the Latter Seven Masters of the time, who highly esteemed prose of the Qin and Han dynasties and poetry of the golden Tang era. The Gong'an School emphasized that literature and art flow forth from the heart, value freedom and originality, and refuse to be bound by any convention. This school urged poets to defy any restriction imposed on them. This view was important to the assertion of individuality and rebellion against tradition, at a time when reverence for and emulation of ancient literature was the trend. It exerted a positive influence on literary creation in that era and later.

引例 Citations:

◎大都独抒性灵，不拘格套，非从自己胸臆流出，不肯下笔。有时情与境会，顷刻千言，如水东注，令人夺魂。（袁宏道《叙小修诗》）

（[他的诗]大都抒发自己真实独特的性情，不拘泥于任何格式套路。只要不是出自本心，绝不肯下笔。有时自己的情感与客观景物融合一片，顷刻成篇，就像大河东流一样，读之夺人心魄。）

Most of his poems express his inner self, without being constrained by any particular regulations or formulas. He would not commit to paper anything not flowing naturally from his inner world. Once his inner feelings and external objects merge into one, words would pour forth to form a magnificent whole, just as a great river flows east undeterred. Readers will be enthralled when reading his works. (Yuan Hongdao: Preface to Xiaoxiu's Poetry)

◎性之所安，殆不可强，率性而行，是谓真人。（袁宏道《识（zhì）张幼于箴铭后》）

（人的性情所形成的习性，大概是不会勉强改变的，只要遵循自己的性情行事做人，就是真性情的人。）

A man's habitual behavior shaped by his own disposition is not quite likely to change. So long as he pursues his true self in his conduct of affairs, he is a true man. (Yuan Hongdao: A Postscript to Zhang Youyu's Admonitory Epigraph)

◎凡诗之传者，都是性灵，不关堆垛。（袁枚《随园诗话》卷五）

（大凡诗歌的流传，都是因为性灵有感染力，与堆砌学识没有关联。）

Poetry spreads far and wide mainly because of its spiritual appeal, not because it is loaded with book knowledge. (Yuan Mei: *Suiyuan Remarks on Poetry*)

兑

/duì/

Dui (Marsh)

"八卦"之一，画为"☱"。"兑"又为"六十四卦"之一，由两个三画的"兑"卦组成，画为"䷹"。在"八卦"系统中，"兑"卦的基本象征意义是水泽。水泽滋养万物，故有悦乐万物之义。"兑"卦由一个阴爻和两个阳爻组成，属于阴卦，在人伦领域象征女性。"兑"卦中的阴爻居于上位，象征家中最小的女儿。

Dui (marsh) is one of the eight trigrams, bundled together in the shape of ☱. It is also one of the 64 hexagrams, composed of two trigrams like this ䷹. In the eight-trigram system, it symbolizes the marsh or lake. The marsh fosters all forms of life, therefore making everything pleasant. The term is composed of one broken line and two unbroken lines. It is considered a yin trigram and a symbol for the female. Since the broken line lies above the two whole lines, it is considered to stand for the youngest daughter of a family.

引例 Citations:

◎兑，说（yuè）也。（《周易·说卦》）

（兑，意为悦乐。）

Dui denotes pleasure. (*The Book of Changes*)

◎丽泽，兑。君子以朋友讲习。（《周易·象下》）

（两片水泽相连，是悦乐之义。所以君子与同门友朋相互讲习学问。）

Dui stands for two connected bodies of water, and represents pleasure. Thus does a scholar engage with like-minded friends in learned disciplines. (*The Book of Changes*)

二谛

／èrdì／

Satyadvaya / Two Truths

两个层面上的真实。“谛”即真实不虚的道理。“二谛”一般指真谛和俗谛，分别又称胜义谛和世俗谛，即在终极本质和世间现象两个层面上各成立一种真实。这一分疏真理的方法始于阿毗达摩类的经典：世俗层面指名言表象，而胜义层面指真实存在的诸法，对应于不同的认知境界。二谛的思想被大乘经典广泛运用，主要指：一切事物在本性的层面上是空，但表现为纷繁的现象（似乎是“有”）。又《中论》言“诸佛依二谛，为众生说法”，其中俗谛指任何名言表诠，包括佛陀的教诲，相应的胜义谛则指超言绝象的真实。基于上述说法，隋代时，释吉藏（549—623）综合各个层面的二谛，发展为“四重二谛”；释智颉（yǐ，538—597）则将空假胜俗二谛与中道相接，统合为“三谛”。

Satya means unfailing truth in Sanskrit. *Satyadvaya* refers to truth at two levels: *paramārtha-satya* (the ultimate truth), which is based on the absolute nature, and *saṁvṛiti-satya* (the conventional truth), based on worldly phenomena. This division of truth according to the level of cognition originates in the canonical *Abhidharma* works, where names, words, appearances, and phenomena belong to the worldly realm, and real dharma belongs to the absolute realm. In the classics of Mahayana Buddhism, *satyadvaya* is widely adapted into the theory that all things, empty in nature, appear as complicated phenomena. (In other words, inherent emptiness appears as *bhava*, or worldly existence.) *Fundamental Verses on the Middle Way* interprets *satyadvaya* in another way. It argues, "The Buddhas teach the dharma to all sentient beings according to *satyadvaya*." The conventional *satya* (truth) refers to all names, words, expressions, and interpretations of worldly phenomena, including the teachings of the Buddha, while the ultimate *satya* refers to the reality beyond word and appearance. This theory influenced a number of Buddhist schools. In the Sui Dynasty, Shi Jizang (549–623), the founder of the Three-treatise School, developed the theory into "the four levels of *satyadvaya*." Shi Zhiyi (538–597), the founder of the Tiantai School, proposed a theory of "the three truths" by incorporating the middle-way truth to the existing theory of the empty truth (or the ultimate truth) and the false truth (or the conventional truth).

引例 Citation:

◎又此即二谛义：真谛空故，不得定有；世谛有故，不得言定无。此用二谛互破其定有、定无也。（释吉藏《中观论疏》卷四（本））

（而且这就是"二谛"的意思：在究竟真实的意义上，事物是空性的，没有持续不变的存在本体；而在世俗现象的层面上，则不能说绝对没有。

这是利用两个层面的真实对两种极端的认识进行互相攻破，否定绝对的有和绝对的无。）

And this is what *satyadvaya* means. According to *paramārtha-satya*, all things are empty in nature, and so there is no constant existence. According to *saṁvṛiti-satya*, all things appear as phenomena, and so there is no absolute nothingness. This is how we use *satyadvaya* to deny constant existence and absolute nothingness. (Shi Jizang: *The Exegesis of Fundamental Verses on the Middle Way*)

法身

/fǎshēn/

Dharmakāya / Body of Dharma

佛法的聚集。“身”义为聚合。佛教常从不同的方面理解觉悟者，而有“二身”“三身”乃至“十身”之说。比如，“色身”或“生身”指具体有形的存在，强调物质的方面；“法身”指无形的、智慧的聚合，强调觉者的本质。此外还有“应身”，特指为了能够教化众生，根据需要变化显现的形式。中国佛教各宗各派对法身的阐释各有千秋，但都重视法身的清净圆满、功用无穷。

Dharmakāya refers to the corpus of the Buddha's teachings. The word *shen* (身 body) means collection in this context. The multifaceted nature of the Buddha inspires the idea of "two bodies," "three bodies," and even "ten bodies." Among them, *rūpakāya* (the body of form or the begotten body) refers to the physical dimension of the Buddha, which features earthliness; *dharmakāya* (the body of dharma) refers to the collection of invisible wisdom, highlighting the inherent nature of the Buddha; and *nirmāṇakāya* (the body of transformation) refers to the doubles of the Buddha who is able to teach the dharma by all means to all sentient beings. Buddhist interpretations on *dharmakāya* vary from school to school, but all of them emphasize its perfect purity and endless functions.

引例 Citations:

◎法身菩萨断结使，得六神通；生身菩萨不断结使，或离欲得五神通。(《大智度论》卷三十八)

（作为法身的菩萨已经断除了各种烦恼，获得了六种神通；而作为生身的菩萨并未断除烦恼，有些远离贪欲的，则有五种神通。）

Bodhisattvas in their body of dharma have eliminated afflictions of all kinds and attained the six types of higher knowledge, while bodhisattvas in their begotten body have not yet eliminated all afflictions. Of the latter, those who stay away from desire may attain five types of higher knowledge. (*The Treatise on the Great Perfection of Wisdom*)

◎然叡公《维摩疏》释云：所谓一法性生身，二亦言功德法身，三变化法身，四虚空法身，五实相法身，详而辩之，即一法身也。何者言其生？则本之法性，故曰法性生身。二推其因，则是功德所成故，是功德法身。三就其应，则无感不形，是则变化法身。四称其大，则弥纶虚空，所谓虚空法身。五语其妙，则无相无为，故曰实相法身。（释澄观《大方广佛华严经随疏演义钞》卷四）

（僧叡的《维摩疏》解释道：所谓第一法性生身，第二功德法身，第三变化法身，第四虚空法身，第五实相法身，仔细考察辨析，其实都是同一个法身。在什么意义上说“生”？因为建立在法性的根基上，所以说是法性所生的法身。其二，推究法身产生的条件，则是由各种善行积累成就的，所以叫功德法身。其三，就法身的感应而言，没有它不能感受的，也没有它不能显现的，所以叫变化法身。其四，为了称扬它的广大，它充斥统摄整个虚空，所以叫虚空法身。其五，为了道出它的微妙，即它自身没有相状、没有造作，所以称其为实相法身。）

In *The Exegesis of The Teachings of Vimalakīrti*, the Buddhist monk Seng Rui explains, “It is said that there are five types of body of dharma: (1) the begotten body of dharma, (2) the beneficent body of dharma, (3) the transformative body of dharma, (4) the empty body of dharma, and (5) the suchness body of dharma. However, if one scrutinizes them closely, one will find out that all these bodies are just different perspectives of the same body of dharma. First, what does ‘begotten’ mean here? Since the essence of dharma begets the body, it is called ‘the begotten body of dharma.’ Second, the body is attained by accumulating beneficence, so it is called ‘the beneficent body of dharma.’ Third, since the body can perceive and manifest everything, it is called ‘the transformative body of dharma.’ Fourth, the body is so vast that it predominates the entire void. Therefore, it is called ‘the empty body of dharma.’ Fifth, the body features extreme delicacy with no form or condition, and so it is called 'the suchness body of dharma.'" (Shi Chengguan: *The Further Exegesis of the Flower Garland Sutra*)

反

／fǎn／

Reversal to the Opposite

相反或复归。“反”用以描述事物在属性或状态上的相反、对立。在此基础上，“反”也指称事物在相反关系中的变化趋向。在这一意义上，“反”包含两种不同的含义：其一，指事物的属性或状态总会在一定情况下向与自身相反的对立面转化。其二，指事物返回到其原初或根本的某种状态或属性。“反”的概念体现着古人对事物内在变化规则的深刻认识。

This term means a reversal to an original and opposite state. By extension, it also refers to the way changes occur in a relationship of opposites. In this sense, the term has two different meanings: one is that a thing's attribute or state will under certain circumstances always transform itself to its opposite; the other is that a thing reverts to its original or fundamental state or attribute. The concept of reversal to an opposite is an expression of the ancient Chinese understanding of the rules governing the way things change.

引例 Citations:

◎反者道之动，弱者道之用。（《老子·四十章》）

（“道”的运动是向对立面的转化或复归，“道”在起作用时总是柔弱处下的。）

The motion of Dao is transforming into the opposite or returning to the original state; and Dao is soft and humble while it is functioning. (*Laozi*)

◎知东西之相反而不可以相无，则功分（fèn）定矣。（《庄子·秋水》）

（知道东西两个方向相互对立又彼此不可缺少，那么就可以确定万物的功用和分位了。）

When we understand that east and west are opposites but cannot exist without each other, then we know the functions and positions of things. (*Zhuangzi*)

方圆

/fāngyuán/

Squareness and Roundness

方形和圆形。“方圆”连用，指事物的形状或性状，亦指使事物“方”或“圆”的方法、规则。古人认为天圆地方，天有旋转、圆通、圆融等特性，地有安静、刚直、方正等特性，主张做人行事应当效法天地的特性，外圆内方，既不放弃内心的坚守，又有适度的融通。在文艺创作特别是书法创作中，古人认为楷书要方，草书要圆，但无论哪种书体都应做到方圆之间的相互依存与和谐统一。

“Squareness,” used in collocation with “roundness,” refers to the shapes and properties of things, or sometimes to the methods and rules of making things square or round. Ancient Chinese believed that heaven is round and earth is square. Heaven revolves, accommodates, and harmonizes. Earth, in contrast, is still, firm, and straightforward. They argued that humans should conduct themselves in imitation of the ways heaven and earth operate, and be “round” on the outside and “square” within, meaning that people should be suitably flexible but firm on issues of principle. In artistic and literary creation, especially in calligraphic creations, ancient Chinese held that regular script should be “square” whereas cursive script should be “round.” However, no matter which type of script is adopted, squareness and roundness should be applied in harmony with each other.

引例 Citations:

◎离娄之明、公输子之巧，不以规矩，不能成方圆；师旷之聪，不以六律，不能正五音；尧舜之道，不以仁政，不能平治天下。（《孟子·离娄上》）

（即使有离娄的好视力、公输般的高超技巧，如果不用圆规和曲尺，也不能画出方形和圆形；即使有师旷的辨音能力，如果不用六律，也不能校正五音；即使有尧舜的方法，如果不施行仁政，也不能治理好天下。）

Even with Li Lou's keen vision and Gongshu Ban's skillfulness, they cannot draw either a square or a round shape without using compasses or a ruler. Even with Shi Kuang's sharp ear for music, he cannot adjust the five notes without using the six pitch-pipes. Even with Yao and Shun's enlightened methods, they cannot run a country well without practicing benevolent governance. (*Mencius*)

◎文有圆有方，韩文多圆，柳文多方，苏文方者亦少，圆者多。（李耆卿《文章精义》）

（文章有的写得圆通，有的写得方正，韩愈的文章大多圆通，柳宗元的文章大多方正，苏轼的文章方正的少而圆通的多。）

The writings of some authors can be round or delicately nuanced, whereas others can be square, or straightforward. Many of Han Yu's essays are round, and many of Liu Zongyuan's are square, while Su Shi's writing is more round than square. (Li Qiqing: *The Essentials of Writings*)

◎方圆者，真草之体用。真贵方，草贵圆。方者参之以圆，圆者参之以方，斯为妙矣。（姜夔《续书谱·方圆》）

（对楷书和草书来说，方圆既是书体又是运用上的一种变化。楷书贵在方正，草书贵在圆通。方正的书体要参照圆通的技巧，圆通的书体要参照方正的技巧，如此才能达到绝妙的水平。）

Squareness and roundness are the core essence and useful complement of regular script and cursive script. The merit of regular script is squareness whereas the merit of cursive script is roundness. Only when squareness is complemented by roundness and roundness is complemented by squareness can true calligraphic excellence be achieved. (Jiang Kui: Subsequent Commentaries on Calligraphy)

防微杜渐

／fángwēi-dùjiàn／

Take Precautions Early

把差错、问题等消灭在萌芽状态。“微”即隐微、不明，指事物尚处于不易被察觉的潜在状态；“渐”即征兆、迹象，指事物刚露出苗头，正缓慢滋长。犹言“防患于未然”。任何事物都有一个由隐而显、由小变大的过程，其间还可能引发其他连锁反应。对于差错、问题等，如果不做好提前防范，及时堵塞各种漏洞，待其大势已成，可能会付出成倍的代价，甚至会酿成全局性灾难。它要求人们深刻认识并精准把握事物演变的内在规律。

This term can also be translated as “nipping the problem in the bud.” Hidden or inconspicuous things are not easily discovered. But there are always warning signs, indications of something newly emerged, slowly developing. All things evolve from hidden to obvious, from small to big, and in time they may lead to harmful consequences. If early steps are not taken to prevent mistakes and problems and to eliminate any defects in time, it will be costly to deal with the consequences, and even disaster may ensue. Thus, people should gain a deep understanding and good grasp of what underlies the evolution of things.

引例 Citations:

◎水旱之灾，虽尚未至，然君子远览，防微虑萌。（《后汉书·郎颉(yǐ)传》）

（水灾、旱灾虽然还没有发生，但有才能的人有远见，能将坏事消灭在萌芽状态。）

Even before flood or drought occurs, a far-sighted and virtuous man will have taken precautions in advance. (*The History of the Later Han Dynasty*)

◎赏刑者，人君之大柄，不可以假人。所以防微杜渐，消逆乱于未然也。（《资治通鉴·晋纪十八·显宗成皇帝咸康六年》）

（奖赏与惩罚是君主手中的两大权力，不能交给别人掌管。这是君主防微杜渐、将祸乱消灭在萌芽状态的保障。）

Rewarding and punishment are two powerful means which the ruler will not concede to others. This enables him to eliminate disasters in bud. (*History as a Mirror*)

◎病之始生，浅则易治；久而深入，则难治。《内经》云："圣人不治已病，治未病。"（徐大椿《医学源流论·防微论》）

（病情刚发生时，不严重，容易治；拖久了，病情加重，就难治了。正如《黄帝内经》上所说："圣明的人不是在发病后才施治，而是在发病前就已经施治。"）

An incipient and light illness is easy to cure. However, prolonged illness is difficult to cure. As said in *The Yellow Emperor's Inner Canon*, the sage begins treatment before, not after, there is serious illness. (Xu Dachun: *The Origin and Development of Illnesses*)

分

/fèn/

Natural Attribute

名分或位分。在一定的秩序之中，事物与他者相区别的属性、状态及其限度，被称为“分”。“分”标志着事物自身的特质，也决定着与他者相区分的界限，如天人之分、公私之分、死生之分等。“分”或源自自然的规则，或取决于人为的命名与规范。就事物或人天生的本性而言，有所谓“性分”之称。而在人伦秩序之中，特定身份所具有的职责，则被称为“职分”。

This may be used to describe either social status or precedence in seniority. In a specific system, or order, it is used to refer to the natural attributes and limitations that differentiate one thing from another. It projects the distinct quality of one thing and at the same time draws the line that marks its difference from others, such as the attributes that differentiate heaven from man, between private and public, and between life and death. It can derive from either natural law or designated titles or standards. As far as the innate character of objects or people is concerned, the term *xingfen* (性分) is used, meaning “different characters between different objects or people.” In human relations, the responsibility for different people of social status is called *zhifen* (职分), meaning the special quality that distinguishes one person’s responsibility from that of another.

引例 Citations:

◎夫名多不当（dàng）其实，而事多不当其用者，故人主不可以不审名分也。（《吕氏春秋·审分（fèn）》）

（事物的名号多与其指称的事物不符，而所行之事也多与其目标的功用不匹配，因此君主不可以不审查事物的名分。）

Many names and titles do not accord with the things they are supposed to represent, and the tasks they carry out do not match what they are supposed to attain. A sovereign ruler must therefore check to ensure all names and titles accord with their attributes. (*Master Lü's Spring and Autumn Annals*)

◎天性所受，各有本分，不可逃，亦不可加。（郭象《庄子注》卷二）

（人和事物所禀受的天性，各有各的内容与限度，不能够逃避，也不能够改变。）

People and objects each have their own natural attributes and limitations, which they cannot ignore or alter. (Guo Xiang: *Annotations on Zhuangzi*)

夫战，勇气也

／fú zhàn, yǒngqì yě／

Fighting Takes Courage.

打仗，凭的是勇气。“勇气”即军队的战斗精神、必胜意志、无所畏惧的气概。它不仅指个体士兵的精神状态，也指整个作战部队的精神气势。它往往是决定战争胜利的必要条件或先决条件。打仗是凶险之事，如果没有足够的勇气，其他任何有利条件都难以发挥应有的作用。其中隐含着这样的军事智慧：在诸多因素中，人的因素第一；在人的诸多因素中，人的精神因素第一。

"Courage" is what it takes to go into a battle. It means the fighting spirit of an army, its will to win and its fearless heroism. The word "courage" not only refers to the spirit of individual soldiers, but also that of the entire army. It is a necessary condition or pre-requisite for winning the victory. Going into battle is dangerous. Without sufficient courage, other favorable conditions will hardly matter. What is implied is the following military wisdom: Of all the factors needed for a victory, the human factor is of primary importance; of all the human factors required, human spirit is of primary importance.

引例 Citations:

◎夫战，勇气也，一鼓作气，再而衰，三而竭。彼竭我盈，故克之。（《左传·庄公十年》）

（打仗，凭的是勇气。头一次击鼓，能振作士气；第二次击鼓，士气就开始衰减了；第三次击鼓，士气就完全没有了。敌方的士气完全没有了，而我们的士气正处在鼎盛阶段，所以就能战胜他们。）

Fighting takes courage. Beating the battle drum for the first time, soldiers will be aroused; the second time it is beaten, they will become less enthusiastic; and the third time, they will lose their fighting spirit completely. As opposed to the enemy soldiers who have lost their fighting spirit, our soldiers are full of it. This is the reason why they can defeat the enemy. (*Zuo's Commentary on The Spring and Autumn Annals*)

◎战而胜者，战其勇者也；战而北者，战其怯者也。（《吕氏春秋·决胜》）

（战胜，靠的是军队的勇敢；战败，多因为军队的怯懦。）

A victory is won because of the valor of an army whereas defeat is suffered due to its cowardice. (*Master Lü's Spring and Autumn Annals*)

高古

/gāogǔ/

Unadorned Antiquity

高远古朴，高雅简古。用于文艺批评，主要指文艺作品中所体现出的意蕴高远古朴、情志高雅，凝重而又深具历史感的艺术风格。“高”体现对空间的超越，不落于现实的具体事物，思想、情感和意愿超然时事和世俗之外；“古”体现对时间的超越，神驰于久远的历史，有拙朴、古雅、凝重的意蕴。“高”和“古”合成一个术语，旨在淡化和超越时代的印记和现实的痕迹，追求一种连接古今、引人追攀又难以企及的意境。它有时也指高人雅士独具的一种人格境界。

This term describes the quality of loftiness or primitive simplicity, and is used primarily in literary criticism to refer to an ancient nobility, an aspiration or sentiment, or an artistic style of historical gravity. “Loftiness” here suggests transcending the limitation of space, not being tied down by concrete objects, thoughts, moods or wishes, and conveys a sense of staying aloof from current affairs and worldly conventions. “Primitive simplicity” here means breaking loose from the confinement of time and traveling back to the remote past. It also implies an unadorned antiquity or austere dignity. By combining these two concepts, the term aims to weaken the imprint of its time and to transcend the bounds of reality, reaching for a normally unattainable realm linking the present to the past. Sometimes, this term is also used to refer to an elevated state of being attained by noble-minded persons.

引例 Citations:

◎畸（qí）人乘真，手把芙蓉。泛彼浩劫，窅（yǎo）然空纵（踪）。月出东斗，好风相从。太华夜碧，人闻清钟。虚伫神素，脱然畦封。黄唐在独，落落玄宗。（司空图《二十四诗品·高古》）

（不同凡俗的人驾御真气，手持莲花升上天界；渡离人间无边劫难，渺然不见其踪影。月亮从东方升起，伴随着清风飞行。华山的夜色葱茏，人们听闻清越的钟声。心灵清虚纯净，超然尘世之外。独自慕尚纯朴的太古时代，洒脱守持道家玄妙的宗旨。）

A man of noble character, with total control over his vital energies, rises up to the heavenly domain, lotus flower in hand. He thus departs from this bitter world of life, making himself totally invisible. The moon rises from the east, sailing across the sky in a fresh breeze. As night falls, darkness closes in on Mount Hua. Clear sounds of bells can be heard. Tranquility reigns deep within, lifting the soul above mortal chaos. This man, in solitary admiration of the charming rusticity of prehistorical times, obeys the profoundly mystical Daoist principle with perfect ease. (Sikong Tu: Twenty-four Styles of Poetry)

◎惟阮籍《咏怀》之作，极为高古，有建安风骨。（严羽《沧浪诗话·诗评》）

（只有阮籍的《咏怀》诗，极显高远古朴的特色，具有建安诗歌的风采骨力。）

Only Ruan Ji's group of poems "Meditations" display an unadorned antiquity, imbued with the vigorous and forceful features of the poetry of the Jian'an period. (Yan Yu: *Canglang's Criticism on Poetry*)

◎汉人诗文，存于今者，无不高古浑朴。（章学诚《文史通义·内篇五·妇学篇书后》）

（汉代人所作的诗文，凡是流传至今的，无不显得高远古雅、浑厚质朴。）

Prose and poetry by Han Dynasty authors, so long as they have survived to this day, all show a lofty adherence to an unadorned antiquity and a charming rusticity. (Zhang Xuecheng: *General Principles of History*)

隔 / 不隔

／gé / bùgé／

Disharmony / Harmony

“隔”指诗文抒情写景不够真切自然，情与景若即若离，让读者产生违和、难以代入的阅读感受；“不隔”指诗文写景抒情真切自然，给读者带来宛如亲见亲历的审美感受。由王国维（1877—1927）在《人间词话》中提出。它传承了古代文艺家以自然为美、注重阅读感受的理念，也受到西方艺术直觉论的影响。直觉关乎艺术经验和心理习惯，有关这对范畴的讨论，表明中西文艺美学思想开始接轨。

“Disharmony” here means an insincere articulation of feeling or an unnatural depiction of scenery. This happens when there is a lack of complete blend of feeling and scenery, causing readers to feel at odds, or unable to identify, with what they are reading. “Harmony,” on the other hand, means a true expression of feeling or a natural depiction of scenery, creating an aesthetic feeling of “being right there to witness.” This pair of contrasting terms was first used by Wang Guowei (1877-1927) in his critical work *Poetic Remarks in the Human World*, where he combines the appreciation of natural beauty and the emphasis on the reading experience favored by ancient China's literati along with the influence of Western notions of artistic intuition. Intuition relates to artistic experience and psychological habit, and discussion of this pair of opposites shows the convergence of Chinese and Western literary aesthetic thought.

引例 Citations:

◎因采菊而见山，境与意会，此句最有妙处。近岁俗本皆作“望南山”，则此一篇神气都索然矣。（苏轼《东坡题跋·题渊明〈饮酒〉诗后》）

（因采摘菊花而看到南山，随意而见的景与悠然自得的心情相通，“见南山”一句最有妙味。近年通行的刻本都写作“望南山”，那全诗的神韵就都索然了。）

While picking chrysanthemums beneath the eastern fence the poet sees the southern mountains – a harmony between the idyllic scenery his eyes casually fall on and a sense of leisurely contentment. “I see the southern mountains” is a most wonderful phrase. However, in recent block-printed editions this has been changed to “I survey the southern mountains” which takes away the charm of the entire poem. (Su Shi: *A Collection of Su Dongpo's Prefaces and Postscripts*)

◎文以意为主，辞以达意而已。古之文不尚虚饰，因事遣辞，形吾心之所欲言者耳，间（jiàn）有心之所不能言者，而能形之于文，斯亦文之至乎？（赵秉文《〈竹溪先生文集〉引》）

（文章以意蕴为主，言辞能够表达意思就可以了。古人的文章不崇尚无意义的修饰，都是根据内容遣词造句，表达我心中想要表达的，偶尔心中有难以用语言传达的意思，但能用文辞表达出来，这也算是达到写作的最高境界了吧？）

It suffices for an essay to convey its author's meaning with well-chosen words. Ancient men of letters disdained empty rhetoric. They chose their words and constructed sentences on the basis of content, free from unnecessary modifiers. Even though they found it hard, once in a while, to articulate themselves effectively, so long as they could lay bare their hearts in words, it was to be the highest attainment in writing. (Zhao Bingwen: A Preface to *Selected Works of Dang Huaiying*)

艮

/gèn/

Gen (Mountain)

"八卦"之一，画为"☶"。"艮"又为"六十四卦"之一，由两个三画的"艮"卦组成，画为"䷳"。在"八卦"系统中，"艮"卦的基本象征意义是山。山峦静止，故有终止、成就万物之义。"艮"卦由一个阳爻和两个阴爻组成，属于阳卦，在人伦领域象征男性。"艮"卦中的阳爻居于上位，象征家中最小的儿子。

This is one of the eight trigrams, bundled together in the shape of ☶. It is also one of the 64 hexagrams, composed of two trigrams like this ䷳. In the eight-trigram system, it symbolizes the mountain. The mountain is still, meaning that everything can be brought to a conclusion and gets what it is supposed to obtain. The term is composed of one unbroken line and two broken lines. It is considered a yang trigram and symbolizes the male. As the unbroken line lies above the two broken lines, it is considered to stand for the youngest son of a family.

引例 Citations:

◎艮，止也。(《周易·说卦》)

(艮，意为终止。)

Gen denotes stopping. (*The Book of Changes*)

◎兼山，艮。君子以思不出其位。（《周易·象下》）

（两山并立，是终止之义。所以君子谋虑之事不超出其分位。）

Gen stands for two mountains side by side, meaning to stop. So what a man of integrity plans to do should never go beyond what his capacity and social status allows him to. (*The Book of Changes*)

公私

／gōngsī／

Public and Private

两种相对的生活领域或行事原则。“公”与“私”大体上包含着两个层面的含义：其一，就生活领域而言，“私”指个人的或个人所属群体之内的生活领域，“公”则是在“私”的界限之外的公共领域。不同生活领域之中存在着不同的秩序原则，彼此之间往往存在冲突。其二，在行事原则的意义上，“私”是以谋求个人或个人所属群体的利益为根本目标的，“公”则是对自私自利原则的超越，体现着天下的公义。

These refer to two different spheres of life and sets of principles for doing things. As far as the spheres of life is concerned, being “private” refers to the life of an individual or group of individuals. Whereas being “public” refers to the public realm beyond these narrow concerns. There are different principles which govern the different spheres of life, and conflict may arise between the two. When it comes to the principles for doing things, it is in the nature of being “private” to pursue the interest of specific individuals or a particular group of individuals, while being “public” means going beyond the selfish or egoistic for the interest of the wider public.

引例 Citations:

◎公私之分明，则小人不疾贤，而不肖者不妒功。故尧舜之位天下

也，非私天下之利也，为天下位天下也，论贤举能而传焉，非疏父子亲越人也，明于治乱之道也。(《商君书·修权》)

（公私的界限分明，则小人不嫉妒贤者，不贤良之人不嫉妒有功业者。因此，尧舜在位统治天下，不是营私以取天下之利，而是为了天下之人而治理天下，选举贤能之人而传承天子之位，并不是疏离自己的儿子去亲近毫不相干的人，而是懂得治乱的道理。）

With clear distinction between public and private spheres, a narrow-minded man does not envy one of virtue, and a mean person has no reason to be jealous of a man of great achievement. Thus Yao and Shun as emperors did not take advantage of their positions to seek personal gain but chose to govern for the benefit of the public. Selecting a man of virtue as successor to the throne did not indicate particular estrangement of father from son, in favor of a person of no blood relations, but instead showed wisdom regarding the ways of good governance. (*The Book of Lord Shang*)

◎己者，人欲之私也；礼者，天理之公也。(朱熹《论语或问》)

（自身所求，体现着人的欲望的自私；礼的要求，体现着天理的公正。）

What a person seeks for his own epitomizes selfish desire; what rite requires represents the justice of heavenly principles. (Zhu Xi: *Questions and Answers on The Analects*)

好生

／hàoshēng／

Cherish Life

爱惜生命，爱惜百姓。中国古人认为，使万物生生不息，是天地的美德；喜爱生存，厌恶死亡，是人之常情。因此，执政者对百姓的生命要多加爱惜，如：不轻易动用极刑，不轻易发动战争，为百姓兴利除害，使百姓安居乐业，等等。“好生之德”是执政者应该具有的美德，也是执政者应该坚守的原则。这一理念与“爱民”“爱人为大”相通，但更进一层，它为治国理政提供了生命哲学基础，它也是人们力行“恕”道、宽以待人的基础理念，中医的人文理论也常以此为基点。

This term means to cherish life and cherish the people. The ancient Chinese believed that the beauty of the natural world lies in its enabling all living creatures to perpetuate themselves, and the universal sentiment of human beings is to cherish life and abhor death. Therefore those who govern must make special efforts to cherish people's lives. For example, they must not readily resort to the death penalty or start wars; they should eliminate things which harm the people and enable people to lead settled lives. The "virtue of cherishing life" is one which those who govern ought to have, and it is also a principle which they should strictly abide by. This concept is consistent with the ideas of "cherishing the people" and that "the greatest good is to cherish others," but it goes a step further. It offers a philosophy of life as a foundation for governance; it is the basic concept explaining why people should be empathetic and accommodating to others; it is also often cited as the starting point for the humanist theories of Chinese medicine.

引例 Citations:

◎天地之大德曰生。(《周易·系辞下》)

(天地的最大德行是使万物生生不息。)

The greatest good in the world is to enable all living things to perpetuate themselves. (*The Book of Changes*)

◎与其杀不辜，宁失不经。好生之德，洽于民心，兹用不犯于有司。(《尚书·大禹谟》)

(与其误杀无罪的人，宁可放过不守常法的人。这种爱惜生命的美德，可以使民心和洽，因此民众就不会触犯刑律了。)

It is better to spare an unruly person than to kill an innocent one by mistake. This virtue of cherishing life will set the people's hearts at ease; hence they will no longer break the law. (*The Book of History*)

◎臣闻天地之于万物也好生，帝王之于万人也慈爱。(《后汉书·寇恂传附曾孙荣》)

（我听说天地对于万物的盛德是好生，帝王对于万民的盛德是慈爱。）

I hear that heaven and earth display goodness to all living things by cherishing life, and kings display goodness to all people through their benevolence. (*The History of the Later Han Dynasty*)

和

／hé／

Harmony

不同事物之间的和谐共处。古人认为，不同事物的共处及事物间稳定秩序的形成，不能通过消除事物之间的差异来实现，而应在尊重和保全个体差异的基础上，寻求事物之间的和谐共处，这就叫“和”。在“和”的状态下，不同事物可以发挥其各自的特质，相互补充、相互辅助，激发个体乃至整体的活力。

The ancient Chinese believed that coexistence of different things and a stable order among them could not be realized by eliminating their differences; such coexistence could be achieved only by seeking to get along in harmony on the basis of respecting and preserving individual differences. That is what is meant by “harmony.” In such a way, different things can develop themselves while complementing each other, stimulating the vitality of both individuals and all.

引例 Citations:

◎夫和实生物，同则不继。（《国语·郑语》）

（不同的事物相互调和而生成新的事物，只有相同的事物则难以有延续。）

Harmony begets new things; while uniformity does not lead to continuation. (*Discourses on Governance of the States*)

◎君子和而不同，小人同而不和。(《论语·子路》)

（君子与人和谐相处却不会盲目附和，小人盲目附和而不能真正和谐相处。）

A man of virtue pursues harmony but does not seek uniformity; a petty man seeks uniformity but does not pursue harmony. (*The Analects*)

和实生物

/hé shí shēng wù/

Harmony Begets New Things.

不同的事物相互调和生成新的事物。由西周末年的周太史史伯提出。史伯认为，不同的事物在和谐共处中可以相互补充、相互辅助，从而生成新的事物。这一原则体现在政治治理中，即要求为政者保全并发挥不同人、物的特质，从而促进新事物的生成、增益与社会整体的发展。

The notion that harmony begets new things was advanced by Grand Astrologer Shibo in the late Western Zhou Dynasty. He believed different things, when coexisting in harmony, would complement each other and beget new things. When applied to political governance, this concept requires those in power to preserve the particular features of different people and things and allow them to flourish. This nurtures the growth of new things and promotes the development of society.

引例 Citation:

◎夫和实生物，同则不继。以他平他谓之和，故能丰长而物归之。若以同裨同，尽乃弃矣。(《国语·郑语》)

(不同的事物相互调和而生成新的事物，只有相同的事物则难以有延续。用一事物去协和另一事物，称为“和”，因此能丰大发展而万物归附。如果以相同的事物去增补另一事物，用尽则被废弃。)

Uniformity does not lead to continuation; it is harmony that begets new things. Using one thing to complement another is harmonization, which leads to lasting abundance and attracts all things. If a thing is added to another of the same kind, it will be discarded when used up. (*Discourses on Governance of the States*)

甲骨文

/jiǎgǔwén/

Inscriptions on Bones or Tortoise Shells

商周时期用于占卜记事而刻在龟甲或兽骨上的文字，又称“契文”“甲骨卜辞”“殷墟文字”，是中国迄今为止发现的最古老文字，距今有三千多年。甲骨文最初出土于河南安阳的小屯村殷墟，一般认为由晚清金石学家王懿荣（1845—1900）于1899年最早发现。商周时期，王室及贵族上自国家大事，下至私人生活，如祭祀、气候、收成、征伐、田猎、病患、生育等等，无不向上天卜问，以占卜结果决定行止。占卜是国家政治生活中的一件大事，有刻辞的甲骨，会被作为国家档案保存起来。目前已出土的甲骨达十万余片，发现的甲骨文单字约4500个，其中能认识的字约1700个。甲骨文已经有较严密的系统，汉字的“六书”造字法在甲骨文中都有所体现，而且有大批形声字产生。甲骨卜辞也是今天研究商周时期历史的第一手资料。

Such inscriptions include oracles and events recorded on bones or tortoise shells of the Shang and Zhou dynasties. They are also known as “script chiseled out with a knife,” “oracles on bones or tortoise shells,” or “script from Yin ruins.” They are the earliest known characters of ancient China dated more than 3,000 years ago. Inscriptions on bones or tortoise shells were first uncovered from among Yin ruins at Xiaotun Village in Anyang in Henan Province, generally believed to have first been discovered in 1899 by Wang Yirong (1845-1900), a late

Qing epigrapher. In the Shang and Zhou dynasties, royal families and noblemen would consult heaven about anything ranging from state business to trivial affairs in daily life, such as sacrificial rituals, weather, harvesting, war, hunting, illness, and giving birth. It was the answers they thus elicited that determined what course of action to take. Divination was an important part of a country's governance; the bones and tortoise shells with characters inscribed on them would be stored away as state archives. So far, more than 100,000 bones and tortoise shells have been unearthed, about 4,500 characters have been tallied, and of these, about 1,700 have been understood and interpreted. Characters on bones and tortoise shells have become increasingly systemized, with the six ways of forming Chinese characters (namely, pictographs, self-explanatory characters, associative compounds, pictophonetic characters, mutually explanatory characters, and phonetic loan characters) all reflected in them and a large number of pictophonetic characters (or phonograms) that had merged. Oracles inscribed on bones and tortoise shells are also valuable firsthand material for studying the history of the Shang and Zhou dynasties.

引例 Citations:

◎文字之兴，原始于书契。契之正字为“栔(qì)”，许君训为“刻”……

"契"者，其同声叚锴(jiǎjiè)字也。……毛公诂"契"为"开"。"开""刻"义同，是知栔刻又有施之龟甲者。(孙诒让《契文举例·叙》)

(文字的起源，原本从刻写开始。刻写的本字写作"栔"，许慎训释"栔"为刻……"契"是"栔"的同音假借字。……毛传训"契"为开，"开"与"刻"意思是一样的，由此知道文字又有刻在龟甲兽骨上的。)

Writing began by cutting out or inscribing characters on bones or tortoise shells. The Chinese character 栔, according to Xu Shen, means exactly this... And 契 is a phonetic loan character derived from 栔... According to *Mao's Annotations on The Book of Songs*, 契 means the same as 开, which has the same meaning as 刻–to carve. Thus we know that some characters are cut out on bones or tortoise shells. (Sun Yirang: *An Interpretation of Some Characters Inscribed on Bones or Tortoise Shells*)

◎卜辞契于龟骨，其契之精而字之美，每令吾辈数千载后人神往。文字作风且因人因世而异，大抵武丁之世，字多雄浑，帝乙之世，文咸秀丽。(郭沫若《殷契粹编·序》)

(占卜之辞刻在龟甲兽骨上，其刻工之精、文字之美，每每令几千年之后的我辈神往。卜辞文字的风格也因人因时而异，大体上说，国王武丁时期，文字大多雄浑，国王帝乙时期，文字都很秀丽。)

Words of divination, cut out on bones or tortoise shells, are truly admirable for their excellent craftsmanship and fine structures. They fascinate me nonetheless today, although they were the work of several thousand years ago. And they also varied in style from time to time and from person to person. Roughly speaking, the characters of King Wuding's time look majestic whereas those of King Diyi's time look elegant. (Guo Moruo: *An Interpretation of Selected Inscriptions on Bones and Tortoise Shells of the Shang Dynasty*)

兼听

/jiāntīng/

Listen to Both Sides

广泛听取各种意见。“兼”有俱、同时之义。领导者在决策之前，一定要广泛听取各种意见，综合、吸纳其中的合理部分。它被认为是贤明领导者的基本特质之一。它要求领导者站在公正的立场上，无偏无私，虚怀若谷。这样，各方都能畅所欲言，提出合理建议，而领导者也能集思广益，权衡利弊，从而保障决策的正确和施策的畅通。

It means to listen to diverse points of view. Before making decisions, leaders must listen to all kinds of opinions and synthesize them so as to extract the most sensible arguments. That is deemed a basic characteristic of a wise and worthy leader. To do so, a leader must be fair, impartial, and open-minded. Only in this way can the parties concerned speak their minds and make rational suggestions, which, in turn, will enable a leader to benefit from various ideas, weigh the trade-offs, make correct decisions, and ensure their successful implementation.

引例 Citations:

◎兼听齐明，则天下归之。（《荀子·君道》）

（广泛听取意见，能够敏捷明智，天下人就会拥戴他。）

Listen to both sides and it will make one wise and well-informed, thus ensuring a broad support all over the land. (*Xunzi*)

◎上问魏征曰:"人主何为而明，何为而暗？"对曰:"兼听则明，偏信则暗。"(《资治通鉴·唐纪八·太宗贞观二年》)

(唐太宗问魏征:"君主怎么做算贤明，怎么做算昏聩？"魏征回答:"广泛听取各种意见就贤明，偏听偏信就昏聩。")

Emperor Taizong of the Tang Dynasty once asked Wei Zheng, "What behavior will make a king wise or foolish?" Wei Zheng answered, "Listen to all kinds of views will make him wise whereas blindly believing will fool him." (*History as a Mirror*)

◎人主以兼听为美，必本至公。(《宋史·陈俊卿传》)

(君主以广泛听取各种意见为美德，而且必定基于最公正的立场。)

Rulers should have the virtue of listening to all kinds of opinions and must be doing so with the utmost impartiality. (*The History of the Song Dynasty*)

见微知著

/jiànwēi-zhīzhù/

Learn About What Is Forthcoming by Observing Tiny Clues

发现细微苗头，就能知道事物的演变趋势或整体状态。“微”即隐微、不明，指事物尚处于不易被察觉的潜在状态；“著”即显著、明显，指事物的本质已经充分显现或事物的发展已处于充分展开的状态。任何事物都有一个由隐而显、由小变大的过程，其间还可能引发其他连锁反应。做任何事情，都要深刻认识、精准把握事物演变的内在规律，既要着眼全局，又要关注细微处，提前防范可能出现的差错、问题，保障行动顺利进行。其中隐含着对于科学认知的诉求。

By finding tiny signs of change, one is able to learn about trends and developments in the status of things. Tiny things are unobtrusive and hard to notice. But they may later cause very obvious consequences. Everything goes from being hidden to being conspicuous, and from small to large, and other chain reactions may occur in the process. So when doing something, we should fully understand and carefully handle its dynamics. We should see both the big picture and small details, get ready early to address any errors and problems that may arise, and ensure success of the undertaking. This also calls for gaining a good understanding of science.

引例 Citations:

◎纣为象箸，箕子怖……圣人见微以知萌，见端以知末，故见象箸而怖，知天下不足也。（《韩非子·说林上》）

（商纣王制作了象牙筷子，箕子恐惧了……圣人见到细微的事情就知道事物的苗头，见到事情的开端就知道最终的结果，所以见到象牙筷子后箕子就恐惧了，知道全天下的东西都满足不了商纣王的贪欲。）

Seeing that King Zhou of Shang had chopsticks made of ivory, Jizi the sage became fearful... Seeing tiny signs, he knew what would sprout from them; seeing the clues, he could foretell the outcome. Therefore when seeing the ivory chopsticks he was fearful as he knew that all under heaven was not enough to satisfy the King' greed. (*Hanfeizi*)

◎故圣人见微知著，睹始知终。（袁康《越绝书》卷十四）

（所以圣人看到细微的苗头，就能知道事物的演变趋势或整体状态；看到事物的初始情况，就能知道它最终会有什么样的结果。）

Therefore, when the sage sees tiny clues, he knows what is forthcoming; when he observes the beginning, he knows the end. (Yuan Kang: *The History of Yue*)

江西诗派

/Jiāngxī shīpài/

The Jiangxi School of Poetry

中国文学史上第一个有正式名称的诗文派别。它以北宋江西籍著名诗人黄庭坚（1045—1105）的“点铁成金”“夺胎换骨”说为主要创作理念。该流派写诗以吟咏书斋生活为主，崇尚瘦硬奇拗的风格；强调师承前人，或师承前人之辞，或师承前人之意；重视文字的推敲技巧，追求字字有出处。这一创作理念与唐代诗歌追求兴象风神有着明显的不同，它的影响遍及整个南宋诗坛，甚至影响到近代。

The Jiangxi School of Poetry was the first school of poetry and prose with a formal name in Chinese literary history. It took as its core tenets the notions of “turning a crude poem or essay into a literary gem” and “squeezing new life out of an old sponge,” as proposed by Huang Tingjian (1045-1105), a Southern Song Dynasty poet from Jiangxi Province. Members of that school devoted themselves to writing poetry with themes about scholarly life. They championed a vigorously “thin and stiff” style, stressed drawing on the skillful wording or remarkable ideas of their predecessors, and paid close attention to the techniques of writing to ensure that each word used in poetic composition can be traced to its origin. Huang’s notions differed from Tang Dynasty poets’ pursuit of impromptu inspiration, elegant subtlety of inspiring imagery as well as vim and vigor in poetic creation. The Jiangxi School’s influence spread across the poetic community of the Southern Song Dynasty, affecting even early modern-day poetic creation.

引例 Citation:

◎歌诗至于豫章始大出而力振之，后学者同作并和（hè），尽发千古之秘，亡（wú）余蕴矣。录其名字，曰江西宗派，其源流皆出豫章也。（吕本中《江西诗社宗派图》，见《云麓漫抄》卷十四）

（诗歌发展到了黄庭坚时才开始宏大，黄力振诗歌创作，后世学黄的人一并兴起、彼此呼应，诗歌创作的千古秘诀尽被挖掘，再无妙法可言。现在记录下他们的名字，命名为“江西宗派”，因为这一派都起源于江西豫章人黄庭坚。）

It was not until Huang Tingjian's time that poetry started to embrace grandeur. Huang tried hard to boost poetic creation. Poets of later generations, who fashioned themselves after Huang, arose in succession and echoed each other. They solved the millennial mysteries of poetic creation so completely that almost no skill was left unexplored. Hence the term "the Jiangxi School of Poetry" to recognize its founder as a native of Yuzhang, Jiangxi Province. (Lü Benzhong: Branches of the Jiangxi School of Poetry)

金文

/jīnwén/

Bronze Script

金文是商周时期铸刻在青铜器上的铭文，是在甲骨文基础上发展起来的一种文字。古代青铜器的种类很多，一般分为礼器与乐器两大类，乐器以钟为代表，礼器以鼎为代表，故前人将钟鼎作为古代青铜器的总称，因此金文也称为“钟鼎文”。金文应用的年代起于商代，盛行于周代，下至秦灭六国，计有 800 多年。据统计，金文有 3700 多字，其中能认识的字有 2420 个，较甲骨文略多。金文的内容多是关于当时祀典、赐命、诏书、征战、围猎、盟约等活动或事件的记录，反映了当时的社会生活。

Bronze script refers to writings inscribed on bronze ware in the Shang and Zhou dynasties; it was developed from inscriptions on bones and tortoise shells. There were many sub-types of bronze ware in ancient China, but they were roughly under two main categories: sacrificial vessels and musical instruments. Sacrificial vessels were represented by tripod or quadripod cauldrons, and musical instruments, by chimes. Therefore, ancient bronze ware was formerly known as “chimes and cauldrons,” and bronze script used to be called “chime and cauldron inscriptions.” The use of bronze script began in the Shang Dynasty, grew very popular in the Zhou Dynasty, and declined in the Qin Dynasty, lasting over 800 years. Bronze script contained over 3,700 characters, of which 2,420 are now intelligible, slightly outnumbering the intelligible characters on bones and tortoise shells. Bronze script was mainly records of sacrificial ceremonies, bestowals, announcements of decrees, declarations of war, hunting expeditions, and pledges of allegiance. It reflected life in those historical periods.

引例 Citations:

◎郡国亦往往于山川得鼎彝，其铭即前代之古文，皆自相似，虽叵复见源流，其详可得略说也。（许慎《说文解字·序》）

（各郡与诸侯国也常常在山间河边挖出钟鼎彝器，上面铸刻的铭文就是前代的古文，它们的字形都很相似，虽然不能看出文字的流变，但是造字的详情也还大致可以说明。）

Various old bronze wares, with epigraphs of old times inscribed on them, were often excavated from the hills and by the riverside in counties and vassal states. The characters looked quite alike. Although nobody can tell exactly how these characters have changed over time, their formative process is more or less traceable. (Xu Shen: *Explanation of Script and Elucidation of Characters*)

◎夫鼎有铭，铭者，自名也。自名，以称扬其先祖之美，而明著之后世者也。（《礼记·祭统》）

（鼎上面多铸刻铭文，“铭”的意思是给自己留名。给自己留名，实际是为了颂扬祖先的美德，让其堂堂正正地传给后世。）

Epigraphs are often inscribed on tripods to leave a name in history and, further, to extol the virtues of one's ancestors so that their reputations will be proudly passed onto posterity. (*The Book of Rites*)

劲健

／jìngjiàn／

Strength and Vigor

强劲刚健。用于文艺批评，主要指作品所显示出的强劲的生命张力、刚劲的语言和矫健的文思，以及所具有的自由奔放的气势和激荡读者心怀的感染力。它要求作者心境澄明、浩气充盈、内在涵养深厚、情志高远深沉，文思纵横无碍，语言丰富多变，强大的精神力量贯穿整个作品。

This term is used mostly in literary criticism to refer to a vigorous life force, the intensity of language, a burst of literary talent, an overwhelming impact, as well as a powerful appeal to readers' hearts. It requires the author to maintain a lucid mind, be filled with positivity, have abundant self-cultivation, embrace noble ideals, be unbridled in literary expression, possess a variety of styles, and infuse spiritual strength into his whole work.

引例 Citations:

◎行神如空，行气如虹。巫峡千寻，走云连风。饮真茹强，蓄素守中。喻彼行健，是谓存雄。（司空图《二十四诗品·劲健》）

（诗人的神思如同翱翔太空，作品的气势好似长虹横贯。仿佛置身于万丈之高的巫峡两岸，伴随疾风的是驰飞而去的云层。涵养真气，培育刚强；蓄积素朴，守持中正。领悟天道永不止息的刚健法则，这就是诗歌需要积存劲力的道理。）

A poet's musings can be likened to a soaring eagle; a literary work should inspire awe like a rainbow across the sky. He feels as if placed on a steep and lofty cliff overlooking the Wuxia Gorge. Clouds swiftly drift away, escorted by a strong wind. Thus, he cultivates vital energies deep inside him, grows in fortitude, and lives out his simple and unadorned life adhering to the principle of propriety. A poet should fully understand the rules governing the robust, ceaseless operation of heavenly forces and needs to accumulate inner strength to produce truly good poetry. (Sikong Tu: Twenty-four Styles of Poetry)

◎延年为人跌宕，任气节，读书通大略，为文劲健，于诗最工而善书。(《宋史・石延年传》)

（石延年为人豪放不羁，崇尚气节，读书粗通其义，但写文章气势强劲刚健，最擅长诗歌，书法也很好。）

Shi Yannian is vigorous and unrestrained. He prizes moral integrity. When reading a book, all he does is to get a basic understanding of its essential meaning. But when he writes, he writes with vim and vigor. He excels at poetry. His calligraphy is also admirable. (*The History of the Song Dynasty*)

竟陵派

/Jìnglíng pài/

The Jingling School of Literary Writing

明代后期的文学流派。因代表人物钟惺（1574—1624）、谭元春（1586—1637）都是竟陵（今湖北天门）人，故称为竟陵派，又称钟谭派。竟陵派重视作家个人的情性流露、反对复古模拟，与公安派主张相同，但他们又认为以袁宏道（1568—1610）等为代表的公安派作品俚俗、浮浅，因而倡导一种幽深孤峭的作品风格，主张文学创作应抒写“性灵”。竟陵派所宣扬的“性灵”，其实是为了追求新奇深奥、与众不同，而刻意雕琢字句，极力造成幽深孤峭、艰涩隐晦的诗歌风格。竟陵派对晚明以后的反拟古文风和小品文的大量产生有促进之功，但他们的创作题材狭窄、语言艰涩，束缚了这一派的发展。

This was a school of literary creation in the late Ming Dynasty represented by Zhong Xing (1574-1624) and Tan Yuanchun (1586-1637), who were both natives of Jingling (today's Tianmen, Hubei Province). It was also known as the Zhong-Tan School. Like members of the Gong'an School of Literary Writing, the Jingling School valued the showing of a writer's true feelings and character and opposed stubborn emulation of ancient literature. However, they regarded works of the Gong'an School represented by Yuan Hongdao (1568-1610) as slangy and shallow. They advocated a serene and solitary style, arguing that literary creation should express the "inner self." But in fact, such an "inner self" pursues only novelty, abstruseness, and aloofness from ordinary mortals. The Jingling School paid excessive attention to wording, trying to create an atmosphere of solitude and profundity. Members of the school contributed to the resistance of stubborn emulation of ancient literature and the emergence of many refined, informal essays. However, the limitation of subject matter and abstruseness of language restrained their further development.

引例 Citation:

◎惺与同邑谭子元春忧之，内省诸心，不敢先有所谓"学古""不学古"者，而第求古人真诗所在。真诗者，精神所为也。察其幽情单绪，孤行静寄于喧杂之中，而乃以其虚怀定力，独往冥游于寥廓之外。（钟惺《诗归·序》）

（我和同郡人谭元春很担心这种情况，我们在内心反思，不敢先存"学古"或者"不学古"的判断，只是探求古人的诗究竟"真"在哪里。所谓真诗，一定是心神活动的结果。考察这种心神活动，发现它实际是古人幽隐孤寂的情感流露以及在喧杂尘世中所保持的安静独行，它有一种特殊的虚怀和定力，使古人能够独游于苍穹之外。）

My fellow townsman Tan Yuanchun and I share the same worry. Even after much thought, we still hardly dare say whether to emulate ancient literature or not. What we attempt to do is to find out where the "true essence" of old-time poetry lies. True poetry has to be the outcome of spiritual activity. A careful examination of such activity would reveal that it shows the sentiments of ancient people in their reclusion and solitude, as well as the journey they quietly pursued regardless of the noise and bustle of the mortal world. True poetry has a magnanimous mind and quiet confidence; it enabled our ancestors to roam free beyond the horizon. (Zhong Xing: Preface to *The Purport of Poetic Creation*)

绝地天通

／jué dì tiān tōng／

Keep Earthly and Heavenly Affairs Separate

断绝地上之事与上天之事的相互干犯与无序沟通。见于《尚书》与《国语》。“绝地天通”是针对民神杂糅所导致的混乱状态，对神人关系做出的一次重新规范。古人认为，神灵祭祀之事属天，民众治理之事属地。天地两个领域的事务应由专人分别管理，以避免人们任意、无序地与神灵沟通，从而维护神灵的权威及其统摄之下的人世秩序。

The need to keep earthly affairs from heavenly affairs separate was first mentioned in *The Book of History* and the *Discourses on Governance of the States*. This was aimed at countering disorderly interaction between the people and the gods and redefining the relationship between them. The ancient Chinese viewed sacrifices to the gods and spirits as belonging to the heavenly realm while governance of the people was an earthly matter. Heavenly and earthly affairs ought to be managed separately by designated people so as to avoid communication with the gods in an arbitrary and disorderly manner. This would maintain the authority of the gods and the order of the human world under the gods.

引例 Citation:

◎颛顼（zhuānxū）受之，乃命南正重（chóng）司天以属神，命火

正黎司地以属民，使复旧常，无相侵渎，是谓绝地天通。（《国语·楚语下》）

（颛顼接受帝位，于是命令南正重掌管上天之事以负责侍奉神灵，命令火正黎掌管地上之事以负责管理民众，使回复旧日的常法，不再相互干犯，这就是所谓的“绝地天通”。）

After ascending the throne, Zhuanxu ordered Chong, the Regulator of the South, to oversee heavenly affairs and care for the gods, and Li, the Regulator of Fire, was ordered to oversee earthly affairs and care for the people, so as to return to old practices and not have heavenly and earthly affairs intrude on each other. This is called keeping earthly and heavenly affairs separate. (*Discourses on Governance of the States*)

君子谋道不谋食

/jūnzǐ móu dào bù móu shí/

A Man of Virtue Seeks Dao, Not Livelihood.

君子所谋求的是大道的确立与践行，不会去谋求个人生计。“君子”本指统治者和贵族男子，后泛指才德出众的人；“道”指根本的原则、道理等；“食”即饭食，泛指基本的生存资源。君子作为社会精英，应当以“道”的确立与践行为己任。这并不是对君子的苛求，作为君子，他首先想到的不应该是个人的生计，而是自己对社会大众的引领使命。

A man of virtue seeks to establish and practice Dao rather than pursue his own livelihood. Men of virtue originally referred to males from the ruling class and aristocracy, but later referred generally to virtuous and talented individuals. Dao here means fundamental principles and way of life; “livelihood” means basic resources for subsistence. As social elites, men of virtue should take upon themselves to establish and practice Dao. That is not an excessive requirement for them. As men of virtue, they should not put daily necessities at priority. Instead, they should think about the expectations placed upon them as social elites to lead the common folks.

引例 Citation:

◎子曰：“君子谋道不谋食。耕也，馁（něi）在其中矣；学也，禄在其中矣。君子忧道不忧贫。”（《论语·卫灵公》）

（孔子说：“君子所谋求的是大道的确立与践行，而不是个人的生计。耕田种地，可能会饥饿；治学求道，可能得到俸禄。君子担心的是大道不能确立或践行，不担心自己贫穷。”）

Confucius said, “Men of virtue seek to establish and practice Dao rather than pursue their own livelihood. Those doing farming may still suffer from hunger, while those engaged in scholarly studies may end up in official positions. Men of virtue, however, worry about the achievement of Dao or its implementation rather than about their own poverty.” (*The Analects*)

乐生

/lèshēng/

To Delight in Life

乐于生存，乐意活着。想活不想死，乃人之常情。它既是打天下者救民于水火、赢得民心、确立自身正当性的基点，也是执政者必须严守的一条底线：不能让老百姓走投无路，觉得生无可恋。为此，执政者至少应注意两点：要创造一切机会，让百姓得以生存；百姓有难，国家要全力救助。否则，国家、社会的基本秩序不可能维持，更不可能达到有效治理。它是“爱人”“民本”思想的体现，与“好生”异曲同工。

Wanting to live and not to die is only natural. A cardinal principle for those who took power was to save the people from disasters and win their trust. It was also what made governance legitimate. One should not drive the people to desperation so that they lose their will to live. Therefore the ruler should bear two things in mind: create all possible opportunities for people to survive, and when they are in difficulties, the state should do everything to help them. Otherwise basic order in state and society cannot be maintained, to say nothing of effective governance. This is the manifestation of the beliefs “caring for others” and “people first” as well as “cherishing life.”

引例 Citations:

◎凡人恶死而乐生，好德而归利。能生利者，道也。道之所在，天

下归之。（《六韬·文韬·文师》）

（凡是人都厌恶死亡而乐于生存，喜好恩德而趋向利益。能为天下人谋求利益的，就代表了道义。谁代表了道义，天下人就会拥戴谁。）

Everybody wants to stay alive and hates to die, and also loves to be a man of virtue and gains benefits. To win benefits for the people is a just cause to pursue. He who represents justice is loved and respected by the people. (*The Six Strategies*)

◎人不乐生，则人主不尊；不重死，则令不行也。（《韩非子·安危》）

（人民都不想活了，君主也就得不到尊崇了；人们都不怕死了，政令也就得不到推行了。）

If people no longer want to live, how could one expect them to respect the ruler? If people are no longer afraid to die, how could one expect them to follow government orders? (*Hanfeizi*)

◎民不畏死，不可惧以罪；民不乐生，不可观（劝）以善。（荀悦《申鉴·政体》）

（人民不怕死了，靠治罪不可能让他们害怕；人民不愿意活着，靠劝导不可能让他们向善。）

If people are not afraid of death, they cannot be frightened with punishments. If people do not want to live, they cannot be persuaded to behave themselves. (Xun Yue: *Lessons Offered*)

诔碑

/lěibēi/

Eulogy or Inscription Carved on a Stela

古代文体名称，是为有一定成就或德行的逝者撰写的篇幅短小的誉美性传文。“诔”主要叙述逝者的德行，表达作者的哀伤，通常用韵文写作；“碑”是刻在石碑上的文辞，一般分两部分：前半简要叙述逝者的生平，后半则用韵文赞美逝者的功业和品德。南朝刘勰（465？—520）认为，诔碑立传的对象，已经由帝王逐渐延及普通人，立传的目的是让逝者的精神永远不朽。其写作要求是，记载事迹要如实，故应有所选择；评述德行较虚，故可以多加誉美。诔文和碑文是生者缅怀逝者的情感需求，满足每个人追求不朽的心理需求，也有弘扬美德、激励后人的意义，因此要避免轻率为文、简单臧否。

These constitute a genre of short rewriting in ancient times to sing the praise of a meritorious or virtuous deceased person. Such a eulogy, written in rhymed verse, was usually used to recount the deceased person's virtuous deeds and express one's grief over his death. The inscription carved on a stela has two parts, with the first part being a brief account of the life of a deceased person and the second extolling the person's merits and virtues. According to Liu Xie (465?-520) of the Southern Dynasties, this kind of writing was no longer written for emperors and kings only, but was extended to cover ordinary people. The text was written to see that the deceased person's noble character passes down to posterity. It should highlight the person's deeds truthfully and eulogize his fine deeds and virtue. A eulogy or an inscription carved on a stela was written to cherish the memory of the deceased and satisfy the need of those who were alive to seek eternal solace. It should also promote virtue and inspire later generations to excel. So, it should be discreet and proper in its assessment of the deceased person.

引例 Citations:

◎诔者，累也；累其德行，旌之不朽也。（刘勰《文心雕龙·诔碑》）

（"诔"的意思是积累，就是罗列逝者的德行，加以表彰而使之永垂不朽。）

Lei originally meant accumulate, so a eulogy lists a deceased person's meritorious and virtuous deeds and extols him to make him eternal. (Liu Xie: *The Literary Mind and the Carving of Dragons*)

◎夫属（zhǔ）碑之体，资乎史才，其序则传（zhuàn），其文则铭。（刘勰《文心雕龙·诔碑》）

（写作碑文，须有史家的才能。它前面的叙事相当于史传，后面的韵文相当于铭文。）

It requires a historian's talent to write an inscription carved on a stela. Its first half is no different from a biography and its second half, written in rhymed verse, is like an epigraph. (Liu Xie: *The Literary Mind and the Carving of Dragons*)

立中制节

/lìzhōng-zhìjié/

Determine the Proper Way for Expressing Human Feelings

确立适中的人情标准而制定礼仪的节度。出自《礼记》和《荀子》。儒家认为，人的情感需要获得适当的抒发与表达。但是，人情的轻重薄厚存在显著差异。礼对于人情的安顿，需要充分把握人情的差异，选择适中的人情程度作为合礼的标准，并依此对人情的抒发与表达做出节制。

This concept originated in *The Book of Rites* and *Xunzi*. Confucianism believes that human feelings need to be properly expressed. However, there are significant differences in the degree of human feelings. Rules should be established to govern the expression of human feelings based on a full understanding of their differences; and the rules for expressing people's feelings should be developed on the basis of a moderate degree of these feelings.

引例 Citation:

◎将由夫（fú）患邪淫之人与？则彼朝死而夕忘之，然而从之，则是曾（zēng）鸟兽之不若也，夫焉能相与群居而不乱乎？将由夫修饰之君子与？则三年之丧，二十五月而毕，若驷之过隙，然而遂之，则是无穷也。故先王焉为之立中制节，壹使足以成文理，则释之矣。（《礼记・三年问》）

（将依从那些邪恶放纵的人吗？那些人早晨父母去世，到了晚上就忘了。要是依从他们的情感而制定礼仪，那就连鸟兽都不如了，怎么会在一起居处而不悖乱呢？将依从那些举止有度的君子吗？对他们而言，服丧三年，二十五个月就结束了，如同马车从缝隙前飞驰而过。如果按照他们的意愿，则是服丧没有穷尽了。因此先王为人们确立适中的标准而制定礼仪的节度，使人们一达到礼的规定，就可以结束丧礼了。）

Should we tolerate those who are under the influence of depravity? When a parent of theirs dies in the morning, they will forget it by the evening. Were we to follow them, we would be worse than the birds and beasts. How could such people live together with others and not cause disorder? Should we instead follow the example of those who are particular about observing rites? For them, the three-year mourning, actually to be completed in 25 months, passes as quickly as a four-horse team galloping past a crack in a wall. If mourning is conducted the way as they wish, it would go on forever. Therefore the former kings established a proper rite for mourning with a fixed mourning period. Once the mourning period is over, mourning may come to an end. (*The Book of Rites*)

良医不能救无命

／liángyī bù néng jiù wúmìng／

Even a Good Doctor Cannot Save a Doomed Patient.

再好的医生治不好必死之人。任何事物的效力都不是无限的，无论医生的医术多高超，医疗条件多优良，都不可能包治百病，总有一些病是不治之症，总有一些人的生命不能挽回。这是不幸的事，也是无可避免的。人们对此必须理性认知，坦然面对。此语也用来提示人们总是有不可抗力与人力极限的存在。

A doctor, no matter how good he is, cannot cure a fatal illness. No power is unlimited. No matter how skillful a doctor is and how advanced the medical facilities are, it is not possible to cure all diseases. There are always some diseases that cannot be cured and some lives that cannot be saved. This is very unfortunate yet inevitable. People should face the reality rationally and calmly. The expression is also used to remind people of *force majeure* and the limitations of human beings.

引例 Citations:

◎良医能治未当死之人命，如命穷寿尽，方用无验矣。（王充《论衡·定贤》）

（好的医生能救治病不至死的人，如果一个人的寿命确实到了尽头，任何药方都无济于事了。）

A good doctor can only cure those who are treatable. If one is fatally ill, then no medicine can save him. (Wang Chong: *A Comparative Study of Different Schools of Learning*)

◎良医不能救无命，强梁不能与天争。故天之所坏，人不得支。（《后汉书·苏竟传》）

（再好的医生治不好必死之人，再强壮的人不能与上天争高下。所以，如果上天想要让其坏灭的东西，人力是抵挡不了的。）

Even the best doctor cannot save a doomed patient, and even the strongest man cannot prevail against Heaven. Therefore, what is doomed by Heaven is not for man to save. (*The History of the Later Han Dynasty*)

◎死病无良医。（《资治通鉴·周纪五·赧王五十六年》）

（对于必死之病，再好的医生也束手无策。）

Even a good doctor can do nothing about a deadly disease. (*History as a Mirror*)

民勇者战胜

/mín yǒng zhě zhàn shèng/

A Country with Brave People Can Win the Victory.

民众英勇，打仗就会获胜。“勇”作为一种品格，主要是指战斗精神、必胜意志、无所畏惧的气概。它往往是决定战争胜利的必要条件或先决条件。这种品格，不仅军队要具备，广大民众也应具备；民众是赢得战争的社会基础，只有民众也表现出足够的英勇，才能使战争在兵源、物力、财力、精神等各方面得到足够的支持。其中蕴涵着总体战争的观念。

Bravery determines the victorious outcome of a battle. As a trait, bravery refers mainly to the fighting spirit, the will to win, and fearless heroism. It is characteristically a necessary condition or a pre-requisite that decides the victorious outcome of a battle. Such a trait should not only be found in an army, but also in the general public because the latter provides the social support to wage a war. Only from a heroic population can adequate manpower, materials, money, and moral that the war needs be drawn. This term implies the notion of a general war.

引例 Citation:

◎民勇者，战胜；民不勇者，战败。（《商君书·画策》）

（民众英勇，就能战胜；民众怯懦，就会战败。）

A country with brave people will win the war whereas that with cowardly people will lose the war. (*The Book of Lord Shang*)

铭箴

/míngzhēn/

Epigraph and Maxim

古代文体名称，是用来针砭过失、褒扬美德并启发哲思的短文。“铭”指铭文，是刻在器物上用以记功颂德的短文，其载体的神圣性及其垂范后世的意图决定了铭文要有宏大格局和雍容气度。“箴”指箴言，是用以规谏劝诫的警语。“箴”的本义是防治疾病的针石，因此有防范过失的含义。“铭”和“箴”都有警示、激励、扬善戒恶的功能，南朝刘勰（465？—520）认为，这两种文体的共同处在于，所选事例要确切可靠，所说道理要经得起推敲，行文要做到简明而意义深远。

These were two types of writing in ancient times aimed at criticizing errors, upholding virtue, and inspiring philosophical thought. *Ming* (铭), meaning epigraph, is a brief account of merits and virtues inscribed on a vessel. Its sacredness and exemplary nature means such writing should be aspirational and visionary. *Zhen* (箴), meaning maxim, on the other hand, is intended to admonish or warn. In Chinese, it is pronounced as *zhen*, meaning an acupuncture needle, a traditional device for preventing or curing disease. Therefore, a *zhen*, should perform the role of preventing an error. Both *ming* or an epigraph and *zhen* or a maxim aim to admonish people against evildoing, promote virtue and punish vice. In the view of Liu Xie (465?-520) of the Southern Dynasties, both types of writing should offer true and reliable information and convincing arguments and be succinct in wording and profound in significance.

引例 Citations:

◎故铭者，名也，观器必也正名，审用贵乎盛德。（《文心雕龙·铭箴》）

（所以"铭"就是命名，观察器物必须据其实质确定名称，审视功用重在增进美好的德行。）

Thus, *ming*, meaning "inscription" here is equivalent to appellation. When examining a utensil or an artifact, one should name it on the basis of its nature. The purpose of such scrutiny is to promote moral behavior. (Liu Xie: *The Literary Mind and the Carving of Dragons*)

◎箴者，针也，所以攻疾防患，喻针石也。（刘勰《文心雕龙·铭箴》）

（箴，就是针刺，用来批评过错、防止祸患发生的文辞好比治病的石针。）

Zhen here means to perform acupuncture for a curative effect. To offer a maxim is, like using an acupuncture needle, to criticize wrongdoing to prevent a disaster. (Liu Xie: *The Literary Mind and the Carving of Dragons*)

◎夫箴诵于官，铭题于器，名目虽异，而警戒实同。箴全御过，故文资确切；铭兼褒赞，故体贵弘润。其取事也必核以辨，其摛（chī）文也必简而深，此其大要也。（刘勰《文心雕龙·铭箴》）

（箴言是官员在君王面前讽诵的，铭文则是题刻在器物上的，二者的名称虽然不同，但用于警诫其实是一样的。箴言的作用在于防范过失，所以行文要依靠事实、表达要确切；铭文兼有褒扬赞美的作用，因此贵在格局宏大、文字温润。它们所选取的事例都必须可靠，经得起推敲，行文一定简明而意义深远，这是写作箴言与铭文的基本要求。）

Zhen, or maxim, is cited by an official to advise the emperor face to face, whereas *ming*, or epigraph, is inscribed on a vessel. Although different in name, they both perform a function of admonition. *Zhen* is used mainly to prevent an error, so it should rely on factual presentation and be precise in wording. *Ming*, on the other hand, also commends fine deeds, so it should be profuse and elegant in style. All the instances cited should be perfectly reliable and can stand up to close scrutiny. They should be concise and exert a profound social influence. These are the basic rules for writing *ming* or *zhen*. (Liu Xie: *The Literary Mind and the Carving of Dragons*)

念佛

／niànfó／

Buddhānusmṛti / Recollection of the Buddha

忆念佛身。又称“随念”。指能够专注在一个清净对象上的精神训练活动，可归入六念、十随念，包括念法、念僧、念戒、念安般(数息)等。“念佛”是其中运用最广泛的一种。念佛的原理在于通过忆念佛陀的殊胜特质，能够消除杂念，为更加高阶的禅定活动做好准备。念佛的形式各有不同，如诵“南无阿弥陀佛”之类的口称念佛，在净土类的实践当中尤为常见。

The recollection of the Buddha is a mental practice of developing concentration on a pure object. It often comes under such a category as “the six recollections” or “the ten recollections” along with the recollections of dharma, sangha, morality, breathing, and so on. Among them, the recollection of the Buddha is the most common practice of contemplation. It instructs one to recollect the supremacy and rarity of the Buddha so that one can eliminate distraction and prepare oneself for more profound meditation. Such recollection can be carried out in a variety of ways. For example, chanting “Namu Amida Butsu” (literally “I salute *Amitābha*”) is a popular practice of the Pure Land School.

引例 Citation:

◎易行道者，谓信佛语教念佛三昧，愿生净土，乘弥陀佛愿力，摄持决定，往生不疑也。（释智顗（yǐ）《净土十疑论》）

（所谓简易践行的方法，是坚信佛陀所教授的通过忆念佛号而达到三昧的境界，期愿死后往生净土，凭借阿弥陀佛摄持众生的非凡誓愿力，必得往生净土而不怀疑。）

It is a simple way of practice to believe in the teachings of the Buddha that one arrives at samadhi, a state of meditative consciousness, through the recollection of the Buddha and vows to seek rebirth in the pure land. With the super normal power of the vows of *Amitābha*, who guards all sentient beings, one will doubtless be reborn in the pure land. (Shi Zhiyi: Ten Doubts Regarding the Pure Land)

鸟尽弓藏

/niǎojìn-gōngcáng/

When the Birds Are Gone, the Bow Is Stored.

鸟猎尽了，弓就该收起来了。比喻战争结束以后，参与领导战争的文臣武将的战时权力被收回或削减。在古代中国，多发生于国家由战时状态向和平状态转变时期，它在一定程度上保障了中央政权和那些文臣武将的安全，有利于国家常态的恢复和长治久安。后来它多用来比喻事成之后，那些曾经出力建功的人就被抛弃了。

Once the bird hunt is over, the bow should be put away. This alludes to the fact that once a war is over, the wartime powers given to civil and military officials should be revoked or diminished. In ancient China, this often occurred when the country shifted from a state of war to one of peace; to a certain extent, it ensured the security of the central government and the civil and military officials, and was conducive to the resumption of the country's normal and stable governance. In later years, this expression came to mean that after a task was achieved, those who had worked toward its success were abandoned.

引例 Citation:

◎夫高鸟死，良弓藏；敌国灭，谋臣亡。亡者，非丧其身也，谓夺其威、废其权也。（《黄石公三略》卷中）

（高飞的鸟死了，良弓就该收起来了；敌国灭掉了，那些出谋划策的功臣也该消亡了。所谓消亡，不是指杀死他们的生命，而是消除他们的威势、解除他们的权力。）

When the high-flying birds have died, the powerful bow is put away. When the enemy state is destroyed, the strategists are eliminated. Eliminating them does not mean killing them; it means stripping them of their authority and power. (*Huangshigong's Three Stratagems*)

浓淡

/nóngdàn/

Denseness and Lightness

浓淡可用于形容颜色、气味、滋味等的深浅、强弱程度。在文艺领域中，浓淡可指绘画色彩的浓淡，文学语言的华美与简淡，艺术风格的浓艳与清淡以及抒情方式的强烈与平淡等含义。“浓”与“淡”是辩证的存在，比如，中国画的笔墨一向有浓有淡，浓不至于浊秽，淡不至于虚缈，尤其水墨画更注重墨色的浓淡，以表现阴阳、向背、虚实、疏密、远近等。理想的艺术境界是浓淡得宜，其他艺术形式对于浓淡的要求与此一致。

This term is used to describe varying degrees of denseness with regard to color, smell or taste. In the fields of art and literature, it refers to the denseness or lightness of a painting's color, ornateness or plainness of literary language, boldness or restraint in artistic style, or to directness or opaqueness of emotional expression. Denseness and lightness are relative to each other. In traditional Chinese painting, for example, the colors chosen can either be dense or light, but they should not be so dense as to be crude or so light as to be insipid. Ink wash painting pays particular attention to the denseness or lightness of color, aiming to achieve a balance between the two. This implies a harmony between the bright and the shady, the front and the rear views, the tangible and the intangible, density and sparsity, and the long- and short-range views. An ideal painting expects denser and lighter hues to set each other off beautifully. This requirement applies also to other genres of art.

引例 Citations:

◎篇章户牖（yǒu），左右相瞰。辞如川流，溢则泛滥。权衡损益，斟酌浓淡。芟（shān）繁剪秽，弛于负担。（刘勰《文心雕龙·熔裁》）

（篇章好像门窗，左右相互配合。文辞好像河流，水满了会泛滥。衡量内容如何减少或增多，斟酌文辞如何加浓或减淡。删去多余剪除杂乱，使文章减少负累。）

A piece of writing is like the shutters on a window, with the left and right sides balanced and well matched. Wording is like a river – if too full, it will flood. We must weigh to see if it needs abridgements or additions, or if it is too ornate or too plain. Any superfluous part should be deleted and any jumbled mass cleaned up so that the composition may not be weighted down. (Liu Xie: *The Literary Mind and the Carving of Dragons*)

◎此卷寂寥简短，不过数笔，而浅深浓淡，姿态横生，使人应接不暇，盖是其得意笔。（尤袤《跋米元晖〈潇湘图卷〉》）

（这幅画意境静谧萧索、尺幅短小，不过寥寥数笔，但是用墨和着色有浅有深、有浓有淡，云雾、山水等各种姿态纷纷呈现，让人目不暇接，应该是他的得意之作。）

The artistic conception of this painting is tranquil and detached. Although small in size and sketchy, it intersperses stronger and milder hues, and heavier and lighter patches. Clouds, mists, mountains, and rivers present themselves in a variety of ways, keeping the eye busy taking it all in at once. It must be the painter's own favorite piece of work. (You Mao: Postscript to Mi Youren's "Landscape Painting of Hills and Rivers in Hunan")

聘礼

/pìnlǐ/

Pinli (Diplomatic Etiquette and Protocol)

最初指天子与诸侯之间或诸侯与诸侯之间访问、会见的外交礼仪，是古代政治生活中的一项重要礼仪。因出访与受访人的身份、访问的缘由、频次等因素的不同，“聘礼”可区分为朝、聘、问等不同等级的聘问。随着政治形势的变化，“聘礼”后来也泛指国与国或其他相对独立的政治主体之间相互访问的外交礼仪。“聘礼”通过朝见、访问过程中的礼仪设计，规范并彰显行礼之人所代表的不同政治主体的地位及相互关系。聘礼后来也指男女订婚时男方向女方行聘的礼仪。

Pinli, meaning diplomatic etiquette and protocol for the visits by the lords to the king and by one lord to another, is an important part of political activity in ancient China. Depending on such factors as the status of visitor and host and the purpose and frequency of the visits, diplomatic etiquette was conducted at three levels: between two ducal lords ruling different states, involving a ministerial-level envoy, and involving senior officials. As the political conditions changed, *pinli* later also referred to the diplomatic ceremonial for visits involving rulers of countries and other independent political entities. The rules observed when paying tribute to a king and at other visits indicated the status and mutual relationships of the different political entities that were represented by the participants on such occasions. Later on *pinli* came to mean the formalities performed by the man's side when getting engaged to a woman.

引例 Citations:

◎凡诸侯之邦交，岁相问也，殷相聘也，世相朝也。（《周礼·秋官·大行人》）

（凡是诸侯之间的邦交，每年要相互行问礼，隔若干年要相互行聘礼，君主世代交替要行朝礼。）

As for the relations between the ducal states, visits by officials should be exchanged annually, ministerial-level missions sent at longer intervals, and the ducal lords themselves are to pay visits on the occasion of the succession of a new ruler. (*The Rites of Zhou*)

◎聘礼，上公七介，侯伯五介，子男三介，所以明贵贱也。（《礼记·聘义》）

（聘礼规定，上公聘问用七个人传宾主之言，侯伯聘问用五个人，子男聘问用三人，所以用来彰显身份的高低。）

According to diplomatic protocol, a superior duke has seven attendants for a given visit; a marquis or earl has five; and a viscount or baron has three. In this way their ranks are made apparent. (*The Book of Rites*)

千里之堤，溃于蚁穴

／qiānlǐzhīdī, kuìyúyǐxué／

A Dam of a Thousand Miles Can Collapse Due to an Ant Hole.

千里长的堤坝会因小小的蚂蚁洞穴而溃决。比喻细小的隐患，也会酿成极大的灾祸。出自《韩非子》。任何事物都有一个由小变大、积少成多的演进过程，如果期望事物向好的方向发展，就必须消除各种隐患与不利因素，不能因为它的细小而忽视其存在，必须早发现、早遏止。此语以比喻的方式，从反面申明了“防微杜渐”的道理。

This expression from *Hanfeizi* highlights how a minute hazard is capable of developing into a devastating disaster. Everything evolves from small to large or grows from few to many. If achieving a good result is expected, then all kinds of hidden risks and potential dangers must be detected and prevented as early as possible, no matter how negligible they may be. The saying illustrates by analogy the importance of early prevention.

引例 Citations:

◎有形之类，大必起于小；行久之物，族必起于少。故曰：“天下之难事必作于易，天下之大事必作于细。”是以欲制物者于其细也。故曰：“图难于其易也，为大于其细也。”千丈之堤，以蝼蚁之穴溃；百尺之室，以突隙之烟焚。（《韩非子·喻老》）

（有形的事物，一定是由小变大的；时间久远的事物，一定是积少成多的。所以说："天下的难事必定从简易开始，天下的大事必定从细微开始。"因此，掌控事物必须从细微时就着手。所以说："谋划难事要从简易处入手，想做大事要从细微处入手。"千丈长的堤坝会因蚂蚁的洞穴而溃决，百尺高的房屋会因烟囱的缝隙冒出火星而焚毁。)

Any living object grows invariably from small to large while any massive accumulation must have started small far back in time. Therefore, it can be said that any difficult job must begin from the easy part and any enormous undertaking must originate from a tiny beginning. Hence, to keep good control of things at hand, it is important to start with managing their small details. That is the reason why one should "start planning for a hard job with its easy part and start undertaking a big task bit by bit." A dam a thousand miles long can collapse by an ant hole and a building a hundred feet tall can be burned to ashes by fire escaping from a chimney crack. (*Hanfeizi*)

◎故百寻之屋，突直而焚燎；千里之堤，蚁垤（dié）而穿败。古人防小以全大，慎微以杜萌。(《晋书·陈頵（yūn）传》)

（所以，八百尺高的房屋，会因为直通通的烟囱冒出火星而焚毁；上千里长的堤坝，会因为小小的蚁穴而溃决。古人在不好的事物尚处于细微阶段就开始防范，将其遏止在萌芽状态，为的是保全大的方面。)

So a building a hundred feet tall can be burned to ashes by fire escaping from a chimney crack and a dam a thousand miles long can collapse because of an ant hole. Ancient people begin to take precautions when dangers are still negligible and try to eliminate them in their nascent stage so as to protect what matters most. (*The History of the Jin Dynasty*)

巧拙

/qiǎozhuō/

Cleverness and Clumsiness

“巧”是灵巧、聪慧，技艺娴熟精湛；“拙”则是不巧，心思迟钝，技艺笨拙。在艺术领域中，“巧”指文辞、构思、技法等方面的巧妙，其艺术形式修饰性较强。理论家们多重视“拙”，反对刻意工巧。真正的“拙”不是粗劣低级，而是自然天成，是“巧”到极致的浑然状态，看不到斧凿痕迹。但是，“拙”应该是自然而然达成的，如果有意识地追求“拙”，很可能收到相反的效果。“巧”与“拙”相辅相成，尚天然去伪饰，则能达到高妙的艺术境界。

“Cleverness” is a synonym for ingenuity, intelligence or exquisite skills. “Clumsiness,” on the other hand, means awkwardness, dullness of the mind or lacking in skill. In the field of art, “cleverness” refers to an ingenious, effortless state of creation whereby general layout, wording, and writing techniques together are at their natural best. It stresses the ornamental function of artistic form. Many theorists favor the idea of retaining “clumsiness” but oppose deliberate manipulation of skill. “Clumsiness” here isn’t the same as shoddy or of a low grade. It means a perfectly natural state of being, or a piece of writing so excellent by its own right as to lose all traces of artificial ingenuity. However, this “clumsiness” should be attained naturally. If a writer deliberately pursues clumsiness, it will only backfire. Cleverness and clumsiness are complementary to each other. Any pretense should be abandoned in favor of what is natural. Only then can artistic excellence be achieved.

引例 Citations:

◎大直若屈，大巧若拙，大辩若讷。(《老子·四十五章》)

（最直的反而像是弯曲一样，最灵巧的反而像笨拙一样，最好的口才反而像不善言辞一样。）

The truly straight will appear crooked; the truly skillful will appear clumsy; the truly eloquent will appear impeded. (*Laozi*)

◎宁拙毋巧，宁朴毋华，宁粗毋弱，宁僻毋俗，诗文皆然。（陈师道《后山诗话》）

（宁可笨拙不要奇巧，宁可朴实不要华丽，宁可粗放不要细弱，宁可生僻不要俗套，写诗作文都是这个道理。）

Better clumsy than deliberately exquisite, better plain than gorgeous, better coarse than dainty, and better rarely seen than conventional – this applies to both poetry and prose. (Chen Shidao: *Houshan's Understanding of Poetry*)

◎文章不难于巧而难于拙，不难于曲而难于直，不难于细而难于粗，不难于华而难于质。可为智者道，难与俗人言也。（李耆卿《文章精义》）

（文章不难写得奇巧而难在重拙，不难写得曲折而难在直接，不难写得繁细而难在粗放，不难写得华丽而难在淳朴。这个道理可以和聪明人讲，难以告诉俗人。）

The difficulty in writing lies not in cleverness, but in clumsiness; not in being meandering, but in being straightforward; not in being meticulous, but in being crude; and not in being gorgeous, but in being plain. This kind of truth can be discussed only with intelligent people, not with the vulgar. (Li Qiqing: *The Essentials of Writings*)

情以物迁，辞以情发

／qíng yǐ wù qiān, cí yǐ qíng fā／

Feeling Varies with Scenery and Verbal Expression Arises from Feeling.

情志随着自然景物而变化，文辞则由心中的情志而生发。自然物象和社会生活图景激发主体的情志，从而诉诸文字。由南朝刘勰（465？—520）《文心雕龙·物色》提出。该术语揭示了文学构思时主观情志随自然景物和社会生活图景变化而变化的特征。刘勰关于情、物、辞三者的关系论源自哲学和语言学上的言、意、象关系的命题，但有其特殊的内涵：就学术文章和应用文写作而言，先在心中形成意义，然后用合适的言辞表意，即使涉及到某些物象或场景，亦是用言辞说明，目的在于说明既有主旨，通常不会存在意义随事物或场景变化的情况；而文学创作则是表现主观感受的过程，所以会随时根据依外物而变化的感情来安排文辞。刘勰的这一论述既揭示了文学发生的原理，又解释了文学构思的特征，表明了六朝文学的创作自《文心雕龙》开始上升为理论上的自觉。

Natural or societal phenomena trigger a subjective feeling, which in turn expresses itself in words. This term was first raised by Liu Xie (465?-520) of the Southern Dynasties in his critical work on literature and writing, *The Literary Mind and the Carving of Dragons*. It reveals the fact that subjective feeling varies with the changes in natural or societal phenomena. This relation between sentiments, natural or societal phenomena, and verbal expressions originates from the relation between speech, meaning, and phenomena in philosophical and linguistic inquiries, but it has its own peculiar implications. Where academic or practical writing is concerned, meaning takes shape in the mind first, and then it finds expression through words; even when it involves objects or scenery, words are employed to explain and support the existing meaning. In such a process, meaning will not change with external objects or scenery. However, literary creation is a process of expressing subjective feelings; therefore its wording sentimentally varies with external objects or scenery. Liu Xie's observation both reveals the origin of literature and explains the features of literary conception; it made literature conscious of its own subjective status. The Six Dynasties' writings reflect this new trend, as noted by Liu in his *The Literary Mind and the Carving of Dragons*.

引例 Citations:

◎岁有其物，物有其容；情以物迁，辞以情发。（刘勰《文心雕龙·物色》）

（一年四季有不同的景物，每种景物各有不同的形貌；人的感情随着景物变化，文辞则是由心中的感情生发。）

Scenery varies with seasons; each scene features different contours and shapes. Human feeling changes with scenery, with words arising from the bottom of the heart. (Liu Xie: *The Literary Mind and the Carving of Dragons*)

◎人禀七情，应物斯感。感物吟志，莫非自然。（刘勰《文心雕龙·明诗》）

（人具有喜、怒、哀、惧、爱、恶、欲等七种情感，受到外物的刺激而心有所感，心有所感而吟咏情志，所有的诗歌都出于自然情感。）

People have the seven emotions of joy, anger, sadness, fear, love, loathing and desire. He expresses his feelings and aspirations in a poetical way when he is stimulated by the external world and his heart is touched. All poems come from natural emotions. (Liu Xie: *The Literary Mind and the Carving of Dragons*)

劝百风一

／quànbǎi-fěngyī／

Much Blandishment and Little Criticism

描写奢靡生活占主要篇幅，而用于劝谏的文辞仅占很小比例。形容文章的立意本想使执政者警诫，效果却适得其反。西汉文学家扬雄（前53—公元18）认为，司马相如（前179？—前118）创作的辞赋，虽然文章结尾归于劝谏，但由于他在辞赋中着力描写、渲染汉武帝（前156—前87）的奢靡生活，使阅读者的注意力只会为辞赋中描画的帝国宏业所吸引，也由此助长了帝王的奢靡心理，劝谏讽喻的效果并不理想。因此，扬雄对司马相如的辞赋提出了批评。

This term means that an essay dwells too much on the luxurious life of a monarch to the neglect of the author's original intention of admonishing him. In the Western Han Dynasty, writer Yang Xiong (53 BC-AD 18) held that although Sima Xiangru (179?-118 BC) always ended on a note of satirical criticism in his prose-poetry, he devoted too much space to the description and glorification of a monarch's luxurious life, bringing readers' attention to the grand achievements of the empire and feeding the monarch's arrogance, thus impairing the admonitory effect. Therefore, Yang criticized Sima Xiangru for such a style of writing.

引例 Citation:

◎相如虽多虚辞滥说，然要其归引之于节俭，此亦《诗》之风（fěng）

谏何异？扬雄以为靡丽之赋，劝百而风一，犹骋郑卫之声，曲终而奏雅，不已戏乎？（《汉书·司马相如传》）

（司马相如的辞赋虽然有大量假托的文辞与夸张的说法，但其文章的立意还是归于节俭，这与《诗经》的讽谏有什么不同呢？扬雄认为司马相如华丽的辞赋中，描写奢靡生活的文辞占主要篇幅，用于劝谏节俭的文辞不过百分之一，就好像一支乐队一直尽情演奏淫靡的郑卫之音，只在乐曲终了时才演奏一点儿庄严的雅乐，这不等同于游戏吗？）

Despite much ostentation and exaggeration, Sima Xiangru finally focused on the importance of being frugal. So what difference is there between this and nuanced criticism in *The Book of Songs*? Yang Xiong argued that in Sima Xiangru's beautiful writing, descriptions of luxurious life dominated all space except toward the end of the essay, where admonitory words emerged extolling the merit of frugality. This can be likened to a musical band playing the decadent music of the states of Zheng and Wei up until the end of the performance, when the band finally struck up some majestic, elegant notes. Now isn't it a joke? (*The History of the Han Dynasty*)

人伦

/rénlún/

Human Relations

人与人之间的秩序差等及行为准则。“人伦”一词最早由孟子（前372？—前289）提出，指父子、君臣、夫妇、长幼、朋友等五种人与人之间的关系，也称“五伦”。古人认为，此五者构成了社会秩序的基本架构，体现着人们在长幼、亲疏、尊卑等方面的身份差等。在不同的人伦关系中，人们应遵循与其身份相符的行为准则。

This refers to the order or hierarchy of human relations and the codes of conduct for people at different levels of the hierarchy. The term, first coined by Mencius (372?-289 BC), is about five human relationships: those between father and son, between monarch and minister, between husband and wife, between siblings, and between friends. It is also known as the five bonds. Such human relations were considered the basic framework of social order, with precedence of senior over junior, of close relatives over distant ones, and between different social ranks all clearly set. Different codes of conduct were to be followed for different human relations.

引例 Citation:

◎人之有道也，饱食、暖衣、逸居而无教，则近于禽兽。圣人有忧之，使契（xiè）为司徒，教以人伦：父子有亲，君臣有义，夫妇有别，

长幼有序，朋友有信。(《孟子·滕文公上》)

（人之所以为人，吃得饱，穿得暖，住得安逸，如果没有教养，那就和禽兽差不多了。圣人为此而担忧，派契做司徒，教育百姓分辨不同的人与人之间的关系，遵循相应的规范：父子之间有骨肉之亲，君臣之间有公正之道，夫妻之间有内外之别，老少之间有尊卑之序，朋友之间有诚信之德。）

People possess a moral nature. If they are well fed, warmly clad, and comfortably lodged, yet left untaught, they would be no better than beasts. Such was the concern of the sage Shun that he appointed Xie to be the minister of instruction, to teach interpersonal relationships and the corresponding norms: between father and son, there should be affection; between sovereign and minister, righteousness; between husband and wife, attention to their separate roles; between old and young, a proper order; and between friends, honor and trust. (*Mencius*)

人命关天

/rénmìng-guāntiān/

Life Is as Important as Heaven.

人之生死，事关重大。"人命"即人的性命，"天"比喻极其重要的事物。同"人命至重"。中国古人认为，人是天地之间最尊贵的生命存在，而生命属于每个人只有一次，最可宝贵。所以，断案、用兵、行医等，但凡事关人命，都要格外慎重。它体现了尊重人、尊重生命的中华人文精神。

Life and death are of the utmost importance. "Life" refers to the lives of people, and "heaven" means the most important matters. The meaning of this phrase is similar to the expression that "life is of supreme importance." The ancient Chinese regarded human beings as the most exalted form of life in the world. Life is the most precious because each person only has one life. Therefore, in judging cases, using military force, practicing medicine, etc., special caution must be exercised when lives are at stake. This exemplifies the humanistic Chinese spirit of respecting people and respecting life.

引例 Citations:

◎且人命至重，难生易杀，气绝而不续者也，是以圣贤重之。（《三国志·魏书·王朗传附子肃》）

（而且人命至关重要，养活不易但杀死很容易，死了不可能复生，所以圣贤很看重人的生命。）

And human life is of the utmost importance. It is hard to sustain life but easy to kill. The dead cannot come back to life; hence the sages took it very seriously. (*The History of the Three Kingdoms*)

◎人命至重，有贵千金。一方济之，德逾于此，故以为名也。（孙思邈《千金方·序》）

（人命至关重要，比千金还要珍贵。开一个药方，把病人治好，这种恩德超过千金，故我将本书取名为《千金方》。）

Human life is the most important, more valuable than a thousand pieces of gold. Writing a prescription which cures a patient is a good deed which is more valuable than a thousand pieces of gold. Therefore the title of my book is *Qianjinfang* (literally *Essential Formulas for Emergencies Worth a Thousand Pieces of Gold,* shortened as *Essential Formulas for Emergencies*). (Sun Simiao: *Essential Formulas for Emergencies*)

◎人命关天，非同儿戏。（《红楼梦》第六十九回）

（人的生死，事关重大，跟小孩子玩游戏可不一样。）

Life and death are of the utmost importance; they are not children's games. (*Dream of the Red Chamber*)

人心

/rénxīn/

Human Heart / Human Desires

对外物的知觉欲求。“人心”与“道心”对举，见于古文《尚书》、《荀子》等典籍。宋儒特别重视“人心”与“道心”的概念，对其含义进行了解释和发挥。宋儒认为，心的知觉活动包含两类内容：其一，由耳目等身体官能所生发的对外物的欲求，称为“人心”。其二，依循于道德原则的知觉意识，称为“道心”。“人心”源自形体所禀受之气带来的私欲。“人心”的私欲容易过度而造成危害，因此应发挥“道心”的功用，以克服过度的欲望。

The “human heart” here refers to human awareness of outside attractions and desires for such attractions. It is in contrast with consciousness of moral principles, and was used in classics such as the “Old Text” version of *The Book of History*, and *Xunzi*. Confucian scholars in the Song Dynasty attached great importance to both concepts, and had interpretations and expositions about them. It was believed that the conscious mind, or heart involved two aspects. The first is the human desires for the outside world that were aroused by sensory organs such as eyes and ears, which is called *renxin*, or the “human heart.” The second is the consciousness of moral principles, which is called *daoxin*, or the “moral mind.” “Human desires” is brought about by the bodily senses and it is selfish. Therefore, the role of the consciousness of moral principles needs to be allowed full play so that excessive human desires which will lead to harm can be held in check.

引例 Citations:

◎人心惟危，道心惟微，惟精惟一，允执厥中。（《尚书·大禹谟》）

（人心危险，道心隐微，用心应精审专一，诚实秉持中正之道。）

The human heart is beset by danger, while the moral mind is subtle and elusive. Concentration of mind is required for sticking to the path of justice and uprightness. (*The Book of History*)

◎心之虚灵知觉，一而已矣。而以为有人心、道心之异者，则以其或生于形气之私，或原于性命之正，而所以为知觉者不同，是以或危殆而不安，或微妙而难见（xiàn）耳。（朱熹《中庸章句序》）

（心的知觉意识，其实是同一个东西罢了。但"人心"和"道心"被认为有分别，是由于"人心"源自形体所禀受之气带来的私欲，"道心"源自天命之性中的正理，因此认为两种知觉有所不同，"人心"危险而不安定，"道心"隐微而不轻易显现。）

Consciousness and senses from the heart are ultimately the same thing. A distinction, however, may be made between the "human heart" and the "moral mind." This is because the former refers to selfish desires brought about by the bodily senses, whereas the latter comes from heavenly principles of justice. Human desires are dangerous and lead to uncertainty. Consciousness of moral principles is elusive and rarely exhibits itself. (Zhu Xi: Preface to *Annotations on The Doctrine of the Mean*)

人怨伤国

／rényuàn-shāngguó／

People's Grievances Harm the Country.

民心有怨，会伤及国家。“人怨”即民怨，指广大民众对施政不满甚至心怀怨恨。如果广大民众对施政普遍不满或怨恨，说明国家治理中可能存在这样或那样的问题，人民不能安居乐业，社会就容易失序进而引发动乱，对于国家来说这不是好事情。对此，执政者或施政者须及时调整政策，努力使民众心情舒畅，保障国家长治久安。这和“国无怨民曰强国”是一个道理，也可以认为是“民本”思想的体现。

The country will be harmed if the people harbor grievances. "People's grievances" refers to dissatisfaction or even anger among the people over government policies. Broad dissatisfaction or anger among the general public indicates there may be problems of one sort or another in the country's governance. If the people cannot live or work in a settled environment, social disorder can easily arise and lead to uprisings, which would not be good for the country. Under such circumstances, those in power or administration must make timely policy adjustments and work hard to ease the people's feelings, so as to ensure stable and durable governance. This is of the same line of thought as the saying "a country with no resentful people is called a strong country," and it can also be regarded as an example of the concept of "people first."

引例 Citations:

◎民怨则国危。(《韩非子·难一》)

(百姓心怀怨恨，国家就危险了。)

If the people harbor grievances in their hearts, the country will be in danger. (*Hanfeizi*)

◎足寒伤心，人怨伤国。(《素书·安礼》)

(人的脚受寒，会伤及心脏；百姓有怨，会伤及国家。)

If a person's feet are cold, his heart will be harmed; if people feel aggrieved, the country will be harmed. (Huangshigong's Strategies on White Silk)

◎上贪民怨，灾害生而祸乱作。(《汉书·食货志上》)

(执权者贪腐而百姓怨恨，就会发生灾祸和动乱。)

If those in power are corrupt and the people are aggrieved, disasters will occur and disturbances will erupt. (*The History of the Han Dynasty*)

仁者乐山，智者乐水

／rénzhě-yàoshān, zhìzhě-yàoshuǐ／

The Virtuous Love Mountains and the Wise Love Water.

有德行的人喜爱山，有智慧的人喜爱水。山崇高持固，以其深厚而滋养万物，仁者由此联想到平和安静、心怀仁德而欣喜；水奔流不息，以其顺势而周流无滞，智者由此联想到顺势而动、随时应变而快乐。此二句互文见义：仁爱而有智慧的人从自然山水中看到自己的天性和追求，乃至看到自己精神的映照，所以见山水而欣悦。这是君子修养的两方面，是君子比德于山水进而移情山水带来的拟人化的自然之美以及赏会之乐。山水因此联系着人类美好的情感，成为常见的审美意象，而徜徉于山水也成为文人修养身心的重要方式。比德是一种富有中国特色的艺术表现方式和思维方式。

According to this term, a mountain is lofty and steadfast, conserving everything with its infinite forbearance. Thus, a virtuous man feels elated by associating this with poise, serenity and benevolence. Water, on the other hand, runs on incessantly, finding its way around without being deterred by any obstacle. Thus, a wise man feels joyful recalling how water meanders its course and keeps pace with the seasons. These two statements complement each other in meaning. Benevolent and wise people note their own nature and aptitude, even their own spiritual state of being, through mountains and water, hence their happiness at the sight of natural scenery. This represents two aspects of a noble-minded person's self-cultivation. It is a personification of natural beauty and an experience of aesthetic appreciation brought about by comparing virtue to, and empathizing with, mountains and water. Thus, mountains and water are often associated with beautiful feelings and have become a common aesthetic image. Wandering among mountains and streams is also seen as an important way for a man of letters to cultivate himself. This comparison made between virtue and natural scenery is typical in Chinese artistic expression and thought.

引例 Citations:

◎岁寒，然后知松柏之后凋也。（《论语·子罕》）

（每年到了天气最寒冷的时节，才知道松树和柏树是最后凋谢的。）

Only when the year turns deadly cold do we see that pines and cypresses are the last to wither. (*The Analects*)

◎知（zhì）者乐水，仁者乐山。知者动，仁者静。知者乐，仁者寿。（《论语·雍也》）

（有智慧的人喜爱水，有德行的人喜爱山；有智慧的人好动，有德行的人好静；有智慧的人快乐，有德行的人长寿。）

A wise man loves water; a virtuous man loves mountains. A wise man is active; a virtuous man stays peaceful in mind. A wise man is happy; a virtuous man enjoys a long life. (*The Analects*)

如来藏

/rúláizàng/

Tathāgatagarbha / Womb of the *Tathāgata*

一切众生都藏有的成就觉悟的潜能。如来藏为觉悟的可能性提供了本体基础，且在相关经典中，一般认为一切众生都有这种觉悟的潜能，它其实是被淹没的意识本质。由于如来藏与阿赖耶识一样清净圆满，提供了相似的解脱依据，故有时混为一谈。魏晋至隋唐之间，“如来藏缘起”的观念趋于显流，即将如来藏分为真如门和生灭门，前者指寂静的本体，后者指阿赖耶识的作用表象，用以解释性寂的本体何以有缘起生灭的问题。

Tathāgatagarbha refers to the potential to realize the Buddhahood inherent in all sentient beings. As an ontological foundation for Buddhahood, this potential is described in related sutras as the submerged essence of consciousness possessed by all sentient beings. It is sometimes confused with *ālāyavijñāna*, because both of them, pure and perfect, provide bases for freedom. From the late Wei and Jin dynasties to the Sui and Tang dynasties, the study of "the dependent origination of *tathāgatagarbha*" became popular. It suggests that the *tathāgatagarbha* heart of all sentient beings opens two gates: the gate of *tathāta* (suchness) and the gate of generation and destruction. The former refers to the noumenon of tranquility, while the latter denotes the appearance caused by the functioning of *ālāyavijñāna*. This explains the reason why the noumenon of tranquility is capable of arising and being extinguished.

引例 Citations:

◎众生如来藏，犹如岩树蜜，结使尘劳缠，如群蜂守护。我为诸众生，方便说正法，灭除烦恼蜂，开发如来藏。（《大方等如来藏经》）

（众生的如来藏，就像岩树上的蜂蜜一般，被各种烦恼纠缠，仿佛有群蜂守护。我为各类众生，用各种巧计开示正法，灭除蜜蜂般的烦恼，好去打开觉悟的宝藏。）

The *tathāgatagarbha* of all sentient beings gets entangled in afflictions of all kinds, just like the honey on a tree growing among rocks is guarded by a colony of bees. For all sentient beings, I adopt expedient methods to teach the true dharma, to destroy the bees of afflictions, and to uncover their *tathāgatagarbha*. (*Tathāgatagarbha Sutra*)

◎本觉隐显为异：藏识在染，名之隐；藏识在果，名之显。非是先染，后随对治，为净法也。故《胜鬘（mán）》言：隐为如来藏，显为法身。此之体义，非用义也。（释慧远《大乘起信论义疏》上之下）

（觉知的本性有隐显的差异：藏识在染污的状态下，就是隐蔽的；在条件成熟的情况下，就是显现的。并不是识本身原来染污，然后通过对烦恼的对治，才成为了清净的本体。因而《胜鬘》上说：隐蔽的状态称作如来藏，显现的状态就是法身。这里指向的是本体［本体没有染净之别，只有隐显状态之别］，而不是功用。）

The nature of Buddhahood is hidden on some occasions and manifested on others. It is hidden in a state of pollution and manifested when the time is ripe. Some hold that the sentient being's nature is originally polluted and attains purity only after afflictions get eliminated, but this is not true. As is mentioned in *The Exegesis of Sutra on the Lion's Roar of Queen Śrīmālā*, the hidden nature is called *tathāgatagarbha*, while the manifested nature is called *dharmakāya* (the body of dharma). What is referred to here is the noumenon rather than the function. (Shi Huiyuan: *The Treatise on the Awakening of Faith in the Mahayana*)

善败者不亡

/shàn bài zhě bù wáng/

Those Adept at Coping with Defeat Cannot Be Destroyed.

善于应对败局者不会灭亡。用兵打仗，任何一方都不可能保证只胜不败。高超的统帅，不仅要善于把握优势和胜局，还要善于应对劣势和败局。当败局无可挽回时，要尽可能地发挥主观能动性，力争将己方的损失降到最低，避免一败涂地，引发总体性、根本性的动摇、崩溃和覆灭。这一术语体现了在被动中寻求主动的辩证法，在现代社会具有更为广泛的应用。

Those who are adept at coping with defeat cannot be destroyed. No party in a war can always be sure of victory and never be defeated. An outstanding commander must not only be skilled at using his advantages when in a position of strength, he must also be adept at coping with disadvantages when in a position of weakness. When defeat is inevitable, he must take the initiative as much as possible and reduce losses to the minimum, thereby avoiding a catastrophic defeat which could lead to an overall breakdown, collapse and destruction. This expression exemplifies the dialectic of seeking to take the initiative when at a disadvantage; it is even more broadly applicable in contemporary society.

引例 Citations:

◎善师者不陈（zhèn），善陈者不战，善战者不败，善败者不亡。

（《汉书·刑法志》）

（善于用兵的人不轻易布阵，善于布阵的人不轻易攻击，善于攻击的人不容易失败，善于应对败局的人不容易灭亡。）

Someone skilled in warfare will not readily deploy; someone skilled in deployment will not readily attack; someone skilled in attacking cannot be readily defeated; someone skilled in coping with defeat cannot be readily destroyed. (*The History of the Han Dynasty*)

◎故师覆于外而本根不摇者，善败也。（《宋史·尹洙（zhū）传》）

（所以军队虽然在外面打了败仗而国家的根本仍未动摇，这就是善于应对败局。）

Thus if a country's army is defeated away from home and yet its foundation remains unshaken, it is adept at coping with defeat. (*The History of the Song Dynasty*)

善为国者不欺其民

/shàn wéi guó zhě bù qī qí mín/

A Good Ruler Does Not Cheat the People.

好的治国者不会欺骗民众。民众的信任是国家政权建立与巩固的基础和保障。这并不是说国家对民众无秘密可言，而是说治国者应坚守诚信，依法施政，正大光明，取信于民，不可滥用公权力，弄虚作假，欺骗民众，以致失去民众信任，离心背德。这和“民无信不立”是一个道理，是“民本”思想的延伸。

Public trust is the foundation underlying state power. A good ruler does not cheat the people. This does not mean that the state has no secrets from the public. Rather, it means the ruler should keep his promise, govern the state by law, maintain moral integrity, and have the trust of the people. He must not abuse his power, be deceitful and cheat the people. These acts can only cost him popular support. This notion resonates with the principle that “without people’s trust the state will not survive,” and it is an extension of the principle of putting the people first.

引例 Citations:

◎不行不可复者，不欺其民也。……不欺其民，则下亲其上。（《管子·牧民》）

（所谓不做不可重复的事情，就是不可欺骗自己的百姓。……国君不欺骗自己的百姓，百姓就会拥戴国君了。）

Not doing what cannot be done again means not cheating one's people... If the ruler does not cheat the people, he will win their support. (*Guanzi*)

◎信，所以不欺其民也。（《韩非子·难一》）

（守诚信是为了不欺骗自己的百姓。）

Trustworthiness means not cheating the people. (*Hanfeizi*)

◎善为国者不欺其民，善为家者不欺其亲。不善者反之……上不信下，下不信上，上下离心，以至于败。（《资治通鉴·周纪二·显王十年》）

（善于治国的人不会欺骗自己的百姓，善于治家的人不会欺骗自己的亲人。不好的治理者与此相反……治理者与被治理者互不信任，上下离心，最终导致了败亡。）

A ruler who conducts good governance does not cheat the people; just as one who keeps his house in order does not cheat his family. A bad ruler does the opposite... If the ruler does not trust his subordinates, they will not trust him. Loss of mutual trust between a ruler and his subordinates will eventually lead to the disintegration of the state. (*History as a Mirror*)

上工治未病

/shànggōng zhì wèibìng/

Great Physicians Treat Before the Outbreak of an Illness.

高明的医生施治于病发之前。“上工”指高明、上等的医生；“未病”指疾病稍有症候，但尚未真正发作的状态。作为中华医学的重要原则，它要求医者精通病理、医理，对病症、病势、病程等有超强的预见力、判断力和控制力，做到早发现、早预防、早治疗，其核心在于预防——预防疾病的发作，预防疾病的转移、变化与传播。它也是中华卫生医学的基础理念，体现了中国人“未雨绸缪”“防患于未然”的治事智慧。

The best physicians start treatment before the outbreak of an illness. *Shanggong* (上工) means skillful, first-rate doctors; *weibing* (未病) is when the slightest symptoms appear but before the actual onset of an illness. This important principle of Chinese medicine requires a doctor to have a thorough command of pathology and medicine, as well as an exceptional ability to anticipate, judge and manage the signs, nature and course of a disease. This enables early discovery, early prevention and early treatment, the essence of which is prevention – preventing the outbreak, metastasis, development and transmission of a disease. This is a fundamental concept of Chinese health and medicine, an example of Chinese wisdom in "preparing for rain before a storm" and "guarding against disaster before it occurs."

引例 Citations:

◎是故圣人不治已病，治未病；不治已乱，治未乱。（《黄帝内经·素问·四气调神大论》）

（所以圣明的人不是在发病后才施治，而是在发病前就已经施治；不是在动乱发生后才治乱，而是在动乱发生前就已经做好防范。）

Thus the wise begin treatment before the outbreak of a disease, rather than after; they do not quell disorder after it erupts, but take preventative measures before it emerges. (*Yellow Emperor's Internal Canon of Medicine*)

◎上工，刺其未生者也；其次，刺其未盛者也；其次，刺其已衰者也。……故曰上工治未病，不治已病，此之谓也。（《黄帝内经·灵枢·逆顺》）

（高明的医生在发病前就施用针刺，次一等的医生在病情尚未严重时施用针刺，再次一等的医生在病情已经减弱时施用针刺。……所以说，上等的医生在发病前就已经施治，而不是在发病后才施治，说的就是这个意思。）

The greatest physicians apply acupuncture before an illness begins; lesser ones do so before the illness gets serious; still lesser ones do so after the illness begins to subside… That is what we mean when we say that the best physicians start treatment before the disease rather than after. (*Yellow Emperor's Internal Canon of Medicine*)

◎善医者，知病势之盛而必传也，预为之防，无使结聚，无使泛滥，无使并合，此上工治未病之说也。（徐大椿《医学源流论·表里上下论》）

（精通医术的人，知道病势严重时必定会转移，所以预先采取防范措施，避免病气聚集，并且不让它扩散，避免多种疾病同时发作，这是上等医生治未病的基本含义。）

A skillful practitioner of medicine knows that a disease will spread once it becomes serious and takes preventative measures ahead of time; this prevents pathogens from growing and spreading, and prevents the simultaneous emergence of several diseases. This is why we say a great physician treats before an illness. (Xu Dachun: *The Origin and Development of Illnesses*)

上医医国

／shàngyī-yīguó／

Great Healers Heal the Country.

高明的医生可以医治国家的疾病。“上医”义同“上工”，指高明、上等的医生；“医国”指的是治理并消除国家的各种疾患。此语本用来比喻高明的政治家像给人治病一样解决国家治理中存在的各种问题和弊病，现在也用来说明高明的医生，能够凭借自己的一技之长，帮助国家防治重大疾患（如各种传染病等），使百姓的生活福祉得到保障。它隐含两个基本观念：其一，治国与治病在基本原理上有相通之处；其二，医者不仅要有高超的医术，而且要有救助苍生、心怀国家的情怀。

A great healer can treat the ills of a country. Like a "great physician," a "great healer" is a skillful, first-rate doctor; "to heal a country" is to treat and eliminate its various ills. Originally this expression was used to describe how a great statesman resolved the various problems and flaws in a country's governance, in the same way a patient's sickness was treated. It now also describes how the expertise of a great doctor can help a country prevent and control major illnesses (such as infectious diseases), thereby ensuring the well-being of the people. The term encompasses two basic concepts: first, there are parallels between healing a country and healing a disease; second, in addition to possessing outstanding skills, a doctor must have both a desire to save people and a concern for the country.

引例 Citations:

◎上医医国，其次疾人，固医官也。（《国语·晋语八》）

（高明的医生可以医治国家的疾患，次一等的只会医治人的疾患，这本来就是医生的职责。）

The greatest healers treat the ills of a country; lesser ones only treat those of people. This is always the duty of physicians. (*Discourses on Governance of the States*)

◎古之善为医者，上医医国，中医医人，下医医病。（孙思邈《千金方·论诊候》）

（古代擅长治病的医者，高明的医生可以医治国家的疾患，中等的医生可以医治人的疾患，下等的医生只会医治身体上的疾患。）

Among the practitioners of medicine in ancient times, the most skillful treated the ills of the country, less skilled ones treated people, and the least skilled ones treated diseases. (Sun Simiao: *Essential Formulas for Emergencies*)

射礼

／shèlǐ／

Rites of Archery

射箭之礼，是古代人伦生活中的一项重要礼仪。“射”指射箭，是古代学子需要掌握的六种基本技能之一。“射礼”即是按照特定的仪程，安排宾主三番轮射。因射者的身份及礼仪场合不同，“射礼”又有大射、乡射、燕射之别。“射礼”中的射箭活动，除了追求中的（dì）的准度等实际射击效果，也要求射者身体和心态的端正，射的不中则反省自己的身心状态。这种射箭的要求和自省的态度，正符合道德修养的要求。因此，“射礼”除了比较射箭技艺，也具有辅助道德修养的意义。

The rites of archery were an important element in ancient Chinese etiquette. Archery was one of the six basic skills that scholars in ancient China needed to master. For a host and his guests, rites of archery involved three rounds of shooting. Based on the status of the participants and the occasion, there were three kinds of contests: the great contest (*dashe*) hosted by the king and ducal lords to select those to take part in sacrificial ceremonies, local contests (*xiangshe*) between scholars invited by local governors and held on the campuses of state-owned schools, and banquet contests (*yanshe*) hosted by the king or ducal lords when entertaining their officials. In such arrow shooting contests, archers must not only try hard to hit the target, they also needed to maintain the right stance and attitude. If one missed the target, he should think about whether he had maintained the right attitude. These requirements and the search for the cause of failure in oneself were in line with the requirements of moral cultivation. Therefore, in addition to being a contest of shooting skills, archery was important in fostering moral cultivation.

引例 Citations:

◎仁者如射，射者正己而后发；发而不中，不怨胜己者，反求诸己而已矣。（《孟子·公孙丑上》）

（仁者就好比射箭的人一样，射箭的人要首先端正自己的姿势然后发箭；发箭没有射中目标，不埋怨成绩超过自己的人，而是反躬自省而已。）

A virtuous man is like an archer. The archer adjusts himself and then shoots. Should he miss, he is not jealous of those who defeat him. He simply examines himself to find out why he has not won. (*Mencius*)

◎故射者，进退周还（xuán）必中礼，内志正，外体直，然后持弓矢审固，持弓矢审固，然后可以言中，此可以观德行矣。（《礼记·射义》）

（因此射箭之人，进退转身必须符合礼仪的规范，内在心志端正，身体挺直，然后手持弓箭稳定瞄准，手持弓箭稳定瞄准，然后才可以言及射中目标，由此可以观察射者的德行。）

The archer must move in a proper way when stepping forward and back and circling round. He should be focused, keep his body straight, hold the bow and arrow steadily and skillfully. Only then can he start shooting at the target. By observing his movement, one can learn about his moral character. (*The Book of Rites*)

身教

/shēnjiào/

Teach by Example

用实际行动教导人。与“言教”（用语言讲述教导人）相对。本指执政者不要满足于简单的发号施令和言语说教，而要以自身的实际行动，为民众起到道德示范作用，以达成社会治理的目标。与“人治”思想相通。后转为重要的教育理念：教师不仅要用语言讲授知识、教育学生，更要以自己的实际行动，在治学、修德等方面成为学生的表率，以便更好地感化学生，实现既定的教育目标。犹言“以身作则”“为人师表”。

This means teaching by one's deeds as opposed to explaining in words. Originally it referred to a ruler who should not just issue orders and tell people what to do. Rather, he should set an example to his subjects with his own actions as a model of virtue, thereby achieving the goal of good order in society. This has something in common with the principle of "rule by man." Later it turned into an educational concept: Teachers should not only teach their students by words; they should also, in their own actual conduct, be an example to the students in scholarship and cultivation of virtue, so as to guide them and reach the goal of education. There are well-known sayings in China like "making oneself an example" and "to be a model teacher to others."

引例 Citations:

◎子曰："其身正，不令而行；其不正，虽令不从。"（《论语·子路》）

（孔子说："执政者自身行为端正，即使不下命令，事情也能行得通；自身行为不端正，即使三令五申，百姓也不会听从。"）

Confucius said, "If a ruler is upright, he could have things done without giving orders; if he is not, people would not listen to him even if he gives repeated orders." (*The Analects*)

◎化民成俗之道，除却身教，再无巧术。（吕坤《呻吟语·治道》）

（教化民众，形成良好风气，除了以身作则，再没有更好的方法了。）

To lead by example is the only way to enlighten the people and cultivate good social mores. (Lü Kun: *Moan and Groan*)

◎言教不如身教。（《明史·汤开远传》）

（用言语教导不如用行动教导。）

Teaching by words is not as good as teaching by example. (*The History of the Ming Dynasty*)

慎终如始

/shènzhōng-rúshǐ/

Be as Discreet at the End as at the Beginning; Remain Discreet Throughout the Whole Process

结束时要像开始时一样谨慎。意思是，做事情自始至终都应小心谨慎，始终如一。决定事情成败的因素很多，单从主观方面说，成功多取决于人的谨慎与坚持，失败则往往由于人的懈怠和放弃。当事情即将完成，尤其是向好的方向发展的时候，人的心理最易松弛，因而出现疏漏，使事情功败垂成，故须强调“慎”字。“慎”源于诚，“诚”就是认真谨慎地对待自己所担负的事情。

One should be discreet at the beginning and all the way through to finish. Many factors determine success or failure. Generally speaking, discreetness and perseverance are the sure way to success, while negligence and laxity invariably lead to failure. When approaching a successful conclusion in an undertaking, people tend to lose drive and things may fall apart at the last minute. Therefore, we must act with discreetness, a concept that has its root in earnestness. Earnestness means handling things with great care.

引例 Citations:

◎民之从事，常于几成而败之。慎终如始，则无败事。（《老子·六十四章》）

（人们做事情，常在快要成功时遭到失败。结束时也像开始时一样谨慎，事情就不会失败。）

Some people fail when they are close to success. So, as we come to the end, we must be as discreet as at the beginning, and this will ensure success. (*Laozi*)

◎虑必先事，而申之以敬，慎终如始，终始如一，夫是之谓大吉。凡百事之成也，必在敬之；其败也，必在慢之。（《荀子·议兵》）

（做事之前一定深思熟虑，反复告诫自己要认真恭敬，结束时要像开始时一样谨慎，始终如一，这叫做最大的吉祥。大凡任何事情，成功一定由于认真恭敬，失败一定由于轻慢懈怠。）

One should be discreet about undertaking his mission and give full consideration to its execution, an attitude one should take all the way, right from beginning to the end. This is the sure way to success. Being earnest and discreet, and you will succeed. Being neglectful and lax, and you will fail. (*Xunzi*)

声无哀乐

/shēngwú'āilè/

There Is No Such Thing as Joyful or Sad Music.

音乐本身没有哀乐之情，只是可以寄寓和激发情感。由三国时期的嵇康（223—262，或224—263）提出。嵇康将心情、意志与音乐区分开，认为情志由心灵主宰，可以表现为多种音乐形式，作者用音乐所表现的情志不等于听者由音乐所激发的情志，以乐观政的实质是执政者先了解社会状况和民众情志，然后借助音乐进行教化：乐师将正确的道理、健康的情志、美好的理想表现为和谐优美的音乐，使音乐与某种特定的意蕴结合，成为广大受众共同的认定，由此影响人心、改变社会风俗，并进而强化音乐的特定意蕴。“声无哀乐”说启示后世文艺批评家将历史变迁、社会风俗、作者的精神世界与受众的心理接受等多种要素结合起来进行考察，更为合理地认识文艺的本质与功能。

Music itself should not be divided into joyful music and sad music – it can only accommodate or inspire feelings. This idea was first raised by Ji Kang (223-262 or 224-263) of the Three Kingdoms period. Ji held that music should be separated from emotion and aspiration. Emotion and aspiration, he said, are controlled by the soul and show themselves in many musical forms. The feelings or aspirations expressed by a musician are different from those evoked in the listener's heart. The relation of music to the governance of a country is that rulers should first know more about the livelihood and aspirations of ordinary people and then moralize them accordingly. Musicians can incorporate truths, wholesome aspirations, and noble ideals into harmonious and beautiful music, linking music to certain implications cementing among the audience a broad consensus so as to exert positive impact on the popular belief, improve social customs, and in the process further strengthen messages implied in the music. This theory of non-differentiation between joyful music and sad music urges literary critics of later generations to examine a combination of factors such as historical changes, social customs, the inner worlds of authors, and the psychological reception of audiences, and to understand the essence and functions of art and literature more rationally.

引例 Citations:

◎声音自当以善恶为主，则无关于哀乐；哀乐自当以情感，则无系于声音。（嵇康《声无哀乐论》）

（声音原本以好听与不好听为标准，跟人的悲哀与快乐没有关系；人的悲哀与快乐原本是感情受到激发以后产生的，与声音没有直接联系。）

Music should be judged on the basis of whether it sounds pleasant or not. It has nothing to do with men's joy or sorrow. Men's joy or sorrow is evoked by actual events; it should not be directly linked to sounds. (Ji Kang: On

Non-differentiation Between Joyful Music and Sad Music)

◎夫哀心藏于苦心内，遇和声而后发；和声无象，而哀心有主。（嵇康《声无哀乐论》）

（悲哀的情感蕴藏在悲苦的心中，遇到音乐旋律便借助它表现出来；音乐的旋律没有固定的形象，但悲哀的情感则是由内心支配的。）

Sad feeling, buried in a grief-stricken heart, will burst forth through musical melodies. Musical melodies have no fixed form, whereas sad feeling is controlled by the heart. (Ji Kang: On Non-differentiation Between Joyful Music and Sad Music)

诗话

/shīhuà/

Criticism on Poetry / *Shihua* (Story-telling with Song and Speech)

主要含义有二：其一，指评论诗人、诗作、诗派及记载诗人逸事及相关考订的著作，是中国古代诗学文献的一个组成部分。诗话肇始于南朝梁代钟嵘（？—518？）的《诗品》，第一部完整意义上的诗话是北宋欧阳修（1007—1072）的《六一诗话》，南宋严羽（？—1264）的《沧浪诗话》是宋代最负盛名、对后世影响最大的诗话。此后，诗话成为评论诗作、发表诗歌创作理论的主要著作形式，明、清两代诗话作品数量巨大，其中以清代王夫之（1619—1692）的《姜斋诗话》和袁枚（1716—1798）的《随园诗话》成就最大。明清时期还刊行了《历代诗话》《历代诗话续编》《清诗话》等，辑集了历代重要的诗话著作。诗话的一般特点是，不追求系统严密的理论体系，主要以评论者的细腻感悟为特色，以若干短句为一则，对诗歌创作中的具体问题或某些艺术规律提出自己的感受和意见。诗话具有较强的文学性和文学欣赏价值。中国诗话以其鲜明的文化特色，有别于西方思辨式的文学理论体系建构和科学严密的语言表述。其二，指中国古代的一种说唱艺术。有说有唱，韵文、散文并用，韵文多为七言诗赞，用于唱；散文即“话”，用于说。现存最早的作品是宋元时期刊印的《大唐三藏取经诗话》。

This term has a two-fold meaning. First, it refers to any work that contains critiques or commentaries on poets, poems, schools of poetry, anecdotes about poets, and textual research. This type of work is a constituent part of scholarly inquiry into classical Chinese poetry. The tradition of offering commentaries on poetry had its origin in "The Critique of Poetry" by Zhong Rong (?-518?) of the Liang Period of the Southern Dynasties. The first somewhat complete commentary on poetry and poets was *Ouyang Xiu's Criticism of Poetry*, by Ouyang Xiu (1007-1072) of the Northern Song Dynasty. The Song Dynasty's most renowned work of poetry commentary, which also had the greatest influence on scholars of later generations, was *Canglang's Criticism on Poetry* by Yan Yu (?-1264) of the Southern Song Dynasty. After that, notes of this kind became a principal medium through which to offer commentaries on poetry and propose theories of poetry composition. The Ming and Qing dynasties boasted the largest number of works of poetry commentary. The best of such works were *Desultory Remarks on Poetry from Ginger Studio* by Wang Fuzhi (1619-1692) and *Suiyuan Remarks on Poetry* by Yuan Mei (1716-1798), both from the Qing Dynasty. During the Ming and Qing periods, *Commentaries on Poetry from Past Dynasties, A Sequel to Commentaries on Poetry from Past Dynasties* and *Qing Dynasty Commentaries on Poetry* were also published, all of which contain important works of poetry critiquing of all dynasties. Commentaries/critiques on poetry essentially shun a comprehensive and elaborate theoretical system and focus instead on articulating the critic's personal, nuanced appreciation and evaluation of poetry. Each of them contains only a few terse remarks, airing views on finer points in poetic composition and revealing personal feelings and thoughts on rules governing artistic creation. Commentaries on poetry are themselves highly literary and deserve to be appreciated from that perspective. Such commentaries on poetry, with their distinctly Chinese cultural features, distinguish themselves from Western scholars' obsession with systematic construction of literary theories and strictly scientific modes of expression.

Second, the term *shihua* may also refer to a kind of age-old art of theatrical performance that intersperse singing with narrative, and verse with prose. Rhymed verse, which normally consists of seven characters to a line, is employed for singing. Prose, on the other hand, is used as in vernacular speech. The earliest extant work of this kind is *Tales of Xuanzang's Journey to the West* compiled and published during the Song and Yuan periods.

引例 Citations:

◎诗话者，辨句法，备古今，纪盛德，录异事，正讹误也。（许顗（yǐ）《彦周诗话》，见何文焕辑《历代诗话》）

（诗话的作用是为了辨析诗歌文法，细述古今流变，记载朝廷盛德，实录奇闻逸事，辨正创作讹误。）

Commentaries on poetry serve to expound rules guiding the composition of poetry, detail the evolution of poetry from past to present, note the imperial court's meritorious deeds, record anecdotes and hearsay, as well as to rectify malpractices in poetic composition. (Xu Yi: *Yanzhou's Commentaries on Poetry*)

◎诗话之源，本于钟嵘《诗品》。（章学诚《文史通义·诗话》）

（诗话的源头，来自于钟嵘的《诗品》。）

The tradition of offering commentaries on poetry is traced back to Zhong Rong's "The Critique of Poetry." (Zhang Xuecheng: *General Principles of History*)

诗家三昧

/shījiā sānmèi/

The Key to Poetic Creation

指诗歌创作的秘诀。“三昧”一词，源于梵文 samādhi 音译，意思是止息杂念、使心神平静，是佛教的重要修行方法，后借指事物的要领、真谛，被诗歌、绘画、书法等各领域借用，成为各领域要领、技巧、秘诀的代名词。“诗家三昧”由南宋著名诗人陆游（1125—1210）在《九月一日夜读诗稿有感走笔作歌》中使用，后用以指代诗歌创作过程中出现的一种灵感突发、文思泉涌的生命状态。陆游在这首诗中讲述年轻时学诗未有心得，后从军，驻守南郑，火热、紧张、刺激的军营生活，使其诗风发生巨变，灵感纷至沓来。从陆游的创作历程可以看出，诗歌来源于生活，“诗家三昧”只有在表现生活、反映现实的创作活动中才能获得。

Sanmei (三昧) originates from the Sanskrit word *samādhi*, meaning “the mental state of being firmly fixed on a single object” or “meditative absorption.” Samadhi used to be Buddhism’s important way to engage in self-cultivation. Later, it took on the meaning of “the gist or true essence of things.” This Sinicized phrase thus made its way into the fields of poetry, painting, and calligraphy and began to be used in the sense of a “knack,” a “trick” or a “secret.” The whole term, “the key to poetic creation,” was first put forward by the Southern Song poet Lu You (1125-1210) in his poem “Poetic Lines Scribbled Down on the Night of the First Day of the Ninth Lunar Month.” Over time, it became used to refer to a burst of inspiration, with words pouring forth like the flow of a spring, in poetic creation. In that poem, Lu You describes how his initial effort to learn to write poetry failed in his youth and how life in the army at Nanzheng, hectic, vibrant, and exciting as it was, thoroughly changed his poetic style and brought forth great ideas. The way Lu You wrote poetry shows that poetry has its origins in life. The inspiration of poetic creation can be drawn solely from the creative activity of reflecting and portraying life through poetry.

引例 Citations:

◎长沙僧怀素，好草书，自言得草圣三昧。（李肇《唐国史补》卷中）

（长沙僧人怀素喜爱草书，说自己悟到了草圣张旭书法的诀窍。）

Huaisu, a Buddhist monk in Changsha, loved the cursive style of calligraphy. He said that he had fortunately captured the key to the calligraphic work of cursive-style master Zhang Xu. (Li Zhao: *A Supplement to Liu Su's Dynastic History*)

◎诗家三昧忽见前，屈贾在眼元历历。天机云锦用在我，剪裁妙处非刀尺。（陆游《九月一日夜读诗稿有感走笔作歌》）

（我突然领悟了作诗的诀窍，屈原、贾谊文章的奥秘在眼前清晰呈现。天赋灵机与云锦般文章全在自己灵活运用，素材选取与文章构思绝非随意尺量刀剪。）

I suddenly captured the key to poetry writing. The secret of success of the poems of Qu Yuan and Jia Yi clearly presents itself before my eyes. Swift inspiration endowed by heaven and truly beautiful writing depend on an author's flexible use of such a knack. The choice of material and structuring of an article should not subject themselves to arbitrary measurement with a ruler or cutting with a pair of scissors. (Lu You: Poetic Lines Scribbled Down on the Night of the First Day of the Ninth Lunar Month)

◎余尝观荆浩论山水而悟诗家三昧，曰：远人无目，远水无波，远山无皴（cūn）。（王士禛《香祖笔记》卷六）

（我曾经从荆浩的山水画论中悟到了写诗的诀窍，他说：画远处的人不可画眼睛，画远处的河不可画水波，画远处的山不可画褶皱。）

I came to see the key to poetic creation through Jing Hao's commentaries on landscape painting. He said: "He who depicts a distant human figure should not try to draw his eyes; he who depicts a distant river should not draw its ripples; he who depicts distant hills, not their folds." (Wang Shizhen: *Notes Written in the Orchid Studio*)

识

/shí/

Vijñāna / Consciousness

其字面义为理解、认识、识见，在佛教当中主要指意识功能。因为它的特殊作用，凡夫对于世界的认识产生了偏差因而导致痛苦，转变这种状态也就要从意识入手。唯识学以世间一切为意识本身的造作，通常被视为一种唯心主义。其意识内部又至少分为见分和相（xiàng）分，即能见和所见的两个方面，因而能够在没有外在世界存在的前提下，提供认知活动的基本条件。其中根据特定的认知对象又分八识：除眼、耳、鼻、舌、身、意六种分别以色、声、香、味、触、法为对象的意识以外，还有末那识和阿赖耶识。第七末那识指恒常思量的功能，一方面为第六识提供依托，一方面将阿赖耶识恒常执持为实有的“自我”。而第八阿赖耶识能含藏业力种子，因而使得一切意识功能处在染污的状态下，与此同时它本身清净的本质却不发生改变。为了解决阿赖耶识这种染净同体的问题，摄论宗另举第九阿摩罗识，即清净识，以区分真妄。

Vijñāna, literally “understanding,” “recognition,” or “knowledge,” refers to the function of consciousness in Buddhism. It distorts a common man’s perception of the world and inflicts mental pain on him. To relieve the pain and restore a correct view, the man has to enhance his own consciousness. Generally regarded as a school of idealism, *Yogācāra*, literally “mind only,” argues that all worldly phenomena are actually shaped by consciousness, which can be divided into at least two parts: the seeing and the seen. Such consciousness is able to lay the foundation for cognition even before the external world exists. According to *Yogācāra*, there are eight types of consciousness based on objects of cognition. The six fundamental types of sensory consciousness of the eyes, the ears, the nose, the tongue, the body, and the mind respectively perceive form, sound, smell, taste, shape, and dharma. The seventh type of consciousness is *kliṣṭamanovijñāna* (deluded consciousness), and the eighth *ālāyavijñāna* (storehouse consciousness). *Kliṣṭamanovijñāna* performs a function of constant reflection, on which the consciousness of the mind is posited. It also persistently conceives *ālāyavijñāna* as the physical self. *Ālayavijñāna*, the repository of the seeds of karma, keeps the purity of all types of consciousness from being contaminated, even though they are in a state of contamination themselves. In order to sort out the entanglement of pollution and purity, the School of the *Mahāyānasaṃgraha* proposes another consciousness, *amalavijñāna* (immaculate consciousness), which distinguishes truth from falsehood.

引例 Citation:

◎识所变相（xiàng）虽无量种，而能变识类别唯三：一谓异熟，即第八识，多异熟性故；二谓思量，即第七识，恒审思量故；三谓了境，即前六识，了境相粗故，及言显六，合为一种。（《成唯识论》卷二）

（意识所变化显现的相状虽可分为无数种，但就其能造作变化的意识功能看只有三类：其一是善恶果报，指第八识，因为它的本质多是因缘异时成熟的结果；其二是思量，即第七识，因为它恒常地审思度量；其三是了别对象，即前六识，因为它们能够分别感官认识的对象，虽然可以说显现为六种不同的形式，但其实是同一种功能。）

Although consciousness appears in numerous forms, there are only three categories of them in terms of function: (1) consciousness of karma execution, which constitutes the essence of the eighth type of consciousness, (2) consciousness of constant reflection, which refers to the seventh type of consciousness, and (3) consciousness of object recognition and distinction, which includes the first six types of consciousness for their sensory perception. Although six types are found in the last category of consciousness, they actually perform the same function. (*Collected Commentaries to the Perfection of Consciousness-only*)

实相

/shíxiàng/

Bhūtatathatā / True Suchness

指万物如实的状态。由于佛教反对实有论，同时需提供一种关于真实的认识，因此佛教的真实勉强描述为如实的状态，而不是实际存在的事物。实相的观念在大乘佛教中尤受重视，并以万法空性为实相。既然一切没有可以被把握的自性，便没有可以作为实相的内容，而只能以“实相”指称智者能够观察到的实情。

Bhūtatathatā refers to the suchness of all existents. Buddhism rejects ontological claims but still needs to deal with reality. Therefore, Buddhist reality can be roughly described as a state of suchness rather than actuality. *Bhūtatathatā* lies at the core of Mahayana Buddhism, where it is defined as the emptiness of all beings. Since the intrinsic nature of the beings can never be understood, there is nothing behind the concept "suchness." Thus, *bhūtatathatā* refers to the reality that only the pandits can observe.

引例 Citation:

◎譬如真水精，黄物著中则随作黄色，青、赤、白色皆随色变。心亦如是，凡夫人内心想智力故，见诸法异相。观诸法实相，非空非不空，不有非不有。是法中深入不转，无所罣（guà）碍，是名度深法忍。（《大智度论》卷五）

（好比真正的水晶，拿黄色的东西放在当中它就变成了黄色；或是放青、红、白色，水晶都会随之而改变颜色。人的意识也是如此，普通人的意识因为妄想的缘故，只看到事物各自有不同的形象状态。而若理解诸法的如实状态，既非绝对的空也不是不空，既非真的存在也不是不存在。深入佛法的理解而不退转，对于任何事物都没有执著，这就叫做对甚深奥义的持受能力，它能够引致解脱。）

Take a piece of genuine crystal for example. If there is a yellow object inside, it appears yellow; if the object is replaced with a cyan, red, or white one, the color of the crystal changes accordingly. Likewise, the mind of a common man is confined to his own fantasy and intellect, and so he sees different appearances of things. However, things exist in a state of suchness, which means that they are neither absolutely empty nor non-empty and that they are neither really existent nor non-existent. If one studies the teachings in depth and does not regress or adhere to anything, one attains the receptivity to the profoundest message that leads to freedom. (*The Treatise on the Great Perfection of Wisdom*)

瘦硬

/shòuyìng/

Thin and Strong

细瘦而劲硬。“瘦”义为细瘦、不丰满，与“硬”连用，侧重指作品的骨力。用于诗歌创作，主要指少铺陈，不堆砌华美的辞藻，不做细腻柔媚的描写，而通过峭拔新奇的声律、刚劲简洁的词句，达成瘦硬的艺术风格；用于书法绘画，主要指笔触细瘦遒劲，具有刚劲挺拔的气质，但又不同于雄浑风格为主的刚健气质。

As employed in traditional Chinese art and literature, “thin” here means bony or not plump; it is used in collocation with “strong,” emphasizing a work’s strong structural force. Used in poetic composition, the term refers to a layout devoid of elaborate writing, flowery wording or excessively subtle description. Instead, amazingly new metrical patterns and bold, concise phrases and sentences are preferred to achieve a “thin and strong” style. When used in painting and calligraphy, it refers to thin but vigorous strokes executed to highlight a quality of unbending rigidity, unlike other more robust styles.

引例 Citations:

◎书贵瘦硬方通神。（杜甫《李潮八分小篆歌》）

（书法注重细瘦劲硬，方能达到非凡的境地。）

Calligraphy, only when performed with thin and strong strokes, will be truly remarkable. (Du Fu: Ode to Li Chao's Modified Lesser Seal Script)

◎宋子京词是宋初体，张子野始创瘦硬之体，虽以佳句互相称美，其实趣尚不同。（刘熙载《艺概·词曲概》）

（宋祁的词作反映宋朝初年的样貌，张先始创细瘦劲硬的词风，虽然他们相互称赞对方的佳句，其实各自的趣味和追求并不相同。）

Song Qi's *ci* poetry reflects the style of the early years of the Song Dynasty, whereas Zhang Xian was the first to create the "thin and strong" *ci* style. Although the two poets praised each other, they differed in artistic taste and pursuit. (Liu Xizai: *Overview of Literary Theories*)

疏密

/shūmì/

Sparsity and Density

由“疏”“密”两个意义相反的词构成，有稀疏与稠密、简略与详细、粗疏与精密、宽松与严密、疏远与亲密等含义。在书法绘画等艺术批评中，疏密主要指结构或布局方面的安排以及笔墨运用的浓淡粗细等。在文学批评中，“疏”与“密”经常联用，“疏”义为疏荡、疏阔、粗略等，多指诗文创作中的随意、粗疏、不严密；“密”义为精密、严密、紧凑等，多指诗文创作中在构思、逻辑、用语等方面严谨周密，有时亦指密集堆砌的毛病。中国古人认为，“疏”与“密”对立统一，好的作品在结构、布局上应当疏密相间。

This concept consists of several pairs of opposites: sparsity and density, brevity and thoroughness, roughness and precision, flexibility and rigor, and estrangement and intimacy. In the artistic criticism of painting and calligraphy, the term is used to mainly describe the structural arrangement, general layout, as well as dark or light, thick or thin execution of strokes in these two art forms. In literary criticism, "sparsity" and "density" often occur together. "Sparsity" means carefree, rough or sketchy. It refers especially to thoughtlessness, carefreeness or looseness in the creation of prose and poetry. "Density" means meticulous, tight or compact. It often refers to rigor and thoroughness in theme development, logic, and wording in the creation of prose and poetry, and occasionally to the demerit of piling too many words up for no good reason. Ancient Chinese believed that sparsity and density represent a unity of opposites. A good work of art should balance density with sparsity in both structure and layout.

引例 Citations:

◎试笔成文，临池染墨，疏密俱巧，真草皆得，似望城扉，如瞻星石。（萧纲《答湘东王上王羲之书》）

（[王羲之] 下笔成文，在砚池边蘸墨挥毫，无论是疏朗还是精密都很巧妙，真书、草书都精心写就，其静处如同远观城门，其动处好似瞻望天上的陨星。）

Wang Xizhi wrote swiftly and skillfully, dipping his brush in the concave inkstone from time to time. His calligraphic writing, whether sparingly or densely spaced, looks truly beautiful. Both his regular script and cursive script were written with immense care. In repose, his flow of words can be likened to watching a city gate from far away. In motion, it can be likened to watching a meteorite in the sky. (Xiao Gang: In Answer to Prince Xiangdong for Kindly Presenting Me with a Calligraphic Work by Wang Xizhi)

◎古无真正楷书……至国朝，文征仲先生始极意结构，疏密匀称，

位置适宜。（谢肇淛（zhè）《五杂组》卷七）

（古代没有真正的楷书……到我们明朝，文征明先生才开始致力于书体结构，他的作品无论疏朗、严密都非常匀称，位置适当。）

There was no real regular script in ancient times... It was not until the Ming Dynasty that Wen Zhengming started to explore rules governing the structure of characters in calligraphy. His works feature a perfect balance between sparsity and density. Each stroke is in its proper place. (Xie Zhaozhe: *An Orderly Narration on Five Assorted Offerings*)

◎词贵疏密相间。（陈廷焯《词坛丛话》）

（词的写作贵在疏朗与严密相互交错。）

The merit of *ci* poetry composition rests on the balance of sparsity and density. (Chen Tingzhuo: *Random Remarks on Ci Poetry Creation*)

韬光养晦

/ tāoguāng-yǎnghuì /

Keep a Low Profile

隐己之长，补己之短。“韬”本指剑衣或弓袋，引申为内藏；“光”即光芒、光彩，比喻实力、才华等优长；“韬光”即收敛自己的光芒，指不以自身优长而炫耀、张扬。“养”即修养、培养；“晦”即昏暗不明，与“光”相对，比喻自身的劣势、短处；“养晦”指加强修养，弥补自身不足。此语体现了中国人低调、内敛，注重自我完善和发展的精神气质。

This term means not to publicize one's strong points but make up for one's weak points. *Tao* (韬) means a sword sheath or an arrow box. *Guang* (光) means light, indicating one's capability and talent. *Taoguang* (韬光) means not to advertise one's strong points, and never boast about or show off one's talent or skills. *Yang* (养) means cultivation while *hui* (晦) means dimness, indicating weakness or disadvantage. *Yanghui* (养晦) means to strengthen one's cultivation and offset one's weaknesses. This term shows that the Chinese people uphold modesty, restraint, self-cultivation, and self-enhancement.

引例 Citations:

◎圣人卑谦，清静辞让者见下也，虚心无有者见不足也，见下故能致其高，见不足故能成其贤。（《文子·九守》）

（圣明的人很谦卑，生性清静谦让的人看自己总是很低，虚心而不以为什么都懂的人总看到自己的不足，看自己很低反而能实现更高的目标，觉得自己不足的人反而能成就高尚的品德。）

A noble person is humble. A sedate and modest person always keeps a low profile, and is aware of his own weaknesses. A person who keeps a low profile may be able to reach high goals. A person who is aware of his own weaknesses may be able to accomplish high morality. (*Wenzi*)

◎自顾年老才庸，粗知《易》理，亦急拟独善潜修，韬光养晦。（郑观应《盛世危言·自叙》）

（想到自己上了年纪，才学平庸，粗知《周易》所讲的道理，打算赶快独自潜心修养，隐己之长，补己之短。）

Thinking that I am getting on in age, without much talent, and only have a shallow understanding of some concepts expounded in *The Book of Changes*, I must hurry to cultivate myself, keep a low profile, and make up my own weaknesses. (Zheng Guanying: *Warning Words in a Prosperous Society*)

同胞

/tóngbāo/

Brothers and Sisters of the Same Parents; Compatriots

同胞胎，指同父母所生的兄弟姐妹。犹言亲人、一家人。北宋张载（1020—1077）依据万物皆由天地所生这一观念，提出了“民胞物与”的思想。“同胞”一词由此超越了血亲家族的范围，进而指同一民族或国家特别是具有共同语言和文化的人，有时甚至超越民族、国家等界限，泛指整个人类。它通过对共同的祖先、语言和文化的溯源，唤起并强化人们对自己民族或国家的归属感和认同感，其中所蕴含的平等、博爱观念，可以说是人类共同的精神财富。

This term originally referred to siblings in the same family. On the basis of the belief that all living creatures are created by heaven and earth, Zhang Zai (1020–1077) of the Northern Song Dynasty advanced the view that all people were brothers and sisters and all living things companions. The meaning of the term was thus extended from blood ties to include people of the same nation or state, especially those with a common language and culture. Sometimes the term goes beyond the nation to refer to all of humanity. By tracing common ancestry, language and culture, it rouses and strengthens people's sense of identity and recognition of their own nation and state. Equality and universal love it embodies are a source of inspiration for humanity.

引例 Citations:

◎同胞之徒，无所容居，其故何也？（东方朔《答客难》）

（连亲兄弟都无处容身，这是为什么呢？）

How could it be that one's own blood brothers have no place to live? (Dongfang Shuo: Replies to a Guest's Questions)

◎乾称父，坤称母。予兹藐焉，乃混然中处。故天地之塞，吾其体；天地之帅，吾其性。民，吾同胞；物，吾与也。（张载《西铭》）

（天是父亲，地是母亲。我这样一个小人物，浑然不觉生活于天地之间。所以，充塞天地的［气］构成我的形体，支配天地的［道］构成我的本性。世人都是我的同胞，万物都是我的同伴。）

Heaven is my father and earth is my mother. Even such a little creature like me can find a place in their midst. Therefore, what fills heaven and earth constitutes my body; what governs heaven and earth forms my nature. All people are my brothers and sisters, and all living things are my companions. (Zhang Zai: The Western Inscription)

◎万品不齐，皆吾同胞，皆吾一体，孰非当敬爱者？（袁黄《了凡四训·积善之方》）

（各色人等各有差别，但都是我的同胞，和我同为一体，有谁不是我应该敬爱的呢？）

Although people are different in many ways, they are all my compatriots. They share a common identity with me; how can I not respect and love them? (Yuan Huang: *Liaofan's Four Lessons for the Clan*)

投桃报李

/tóutáo-bàolǐ/

Return Kindness with Kindness / Return Goodwill in Kind

你赠我木桃，我回赠你木李（“木桃”即樝（zhā）子，一种落叶灌木，果实圆，味酸涩，一说即桃子）。泛指互赠礼品，礼尚往来。其意义并不在于互赠的礼品本身，而在于以礼品为载体，传递对对方的善意，表达与对方永结友好的诚意，其中隐含平等互惠的关系原则。它是“以德报德”（相互善待）这一关系准则的形象表达，是“礼尚往来”理念积极面的体现。小到个人关系，大到国家关系，皆循此理。

Toutaobaoli, the Chinese original, literally means when you give me a peach, I will also give you a peach in appreciation. The term generally refers to reciprocating a gift in kind as an expression of mutual courtesy. What is important is not the gift itself but the goodwill conveyed by the gift as well as the desire of forging lasting friendship with the other party. The expression implies the principle of equality and mutual benefit. It is a figurative way to state a principle of "returning good for good," which is a positive aspect of the notion of reciprocity. This principle applies to relationships big or small, ranging from those between individuals to those between states.

引例 Citations:

◎投我以木桃，报之以琼瑶。匪报也，永以为好也！（《诗经·国

风·木瓜》)

(你赠我木桃，我回赠你琼瑶。不是为了回赠物品，而是为了永远结好。)

You gave me a peach and I gave you a beautiful jade in return. It is not for repayment of your gift, but for our lasting friendship. (*The Book of Songs*)

◎《大雅》之所道曰："无言而不雠（chóu），无德而不报。""投我以桃，报之以李。"即此言爱人者必见爱也，而恶人者必见恶也。(《墨子·兼爱下》)

(《诗经·大雅》说："没有出言就没有应答，没有施恩就没有报答。""你赠我木桃，我回赠你木李。"这就是说爱人的人必定会被人爱，而憎恶人的人必定会被人憎恶。)

The Book of Songs has these lines: "Words are said, hence the answers; virtues are rendered, hence the return of kindness." "Give me a peach, and I will give you back a peach." These lines mean that if you love others you will be bestowed with love, but if you hate others you will be treated in the same way. (*Mozi*)

物极必反

/wùjí-bìfǎn/

When Reaching an Extreme, Things Are Bound to Revert to Their Opposites.

事物到达某一极端必然会向其反面转化。古人很早就认识到，事物的属性或状态总会在一定情况下向与自身相反的对立面转化。北宋的程颐（1033—1107）则对这一事物变化的规则做出了更细致的描述，提出了"物极必反"之说。"物极必反"揭示的是事物在属性或状态上发展到极端时的变化趋向。事物在极端状态下，其属性或状态的反向转变是必然发生的。

The ancient Chinese came to know early that the nature or state of things change to their opposite under certain circumstances. In the Northern Song Dynasty, Cheng Yi (1033-1107) gave a detailed description of the rules of such change when he argued that "when reaching an extreme, things are bound to revert to their opposites." This view believes that things tend to change when reaching an extreme in their nature or state. In such a state, things inevitably transform themselves into their opposite.

引例 Citation:

◎物极必返，其理须如此。有生便有死，有始便有终。（《二程遗书·入关语录》）

（事物到达极端就必然向其反面转化，事物的道理就是这样。有生便会有死，有开始就会有终结。）

When reaching an extreme, things are bound to revert to their opposite state. This is the way things work. When there is life there is death, and when there is a beginning there is an end. (*Writings of the Cheng Brothers*)

洗炼

/xǐliàn/

Make Writing Succinct

精简词句，提炼要义。洗炼是一种文字干净、主旨鲜明的文学风格。“洗”指清洗矿石、去除杂质，喻指删除芜杂文字；“炼”指金属的冶炼提纯，喻指提炼文章的精义或本真性情。作为一种写作方式，它包括炼意和炼辞两个方面，较之南朝刘勰（465？—520）的“熔裁”有更明确的要求；作为一种文学风格，它要求文章的词句必须与情志理高度配合而又简明扼要。

This term means that wording should be refined to highlight the essential message. Terseness is a mark of neat and thematically explicit writing. The idea originates from the process of cleansing metal ores for the removal of impurities, or from that of smelting metals. Figuratively, it refers to an authorial effort to capture the core message by cutting out redundant wording. As a way of writing, this involves the refinement of both content and wording; it sets a more clear-cut requirement on writers than the idea of "fusion for greater brevity," which was proposed by Liu Xie (465?-520) of the Southern Dynasties. As a literary style, it calls for full agreement between wording, aspiration, and philosophical thought, as well as for conciseness.

引例 Citations:

◎岂若澡雪灵府，洗练神宅，据道为心，依德为虑，使迹穷则义斯畅，身泰则理兼通，岂不美哉！（《宋书·顾觊之传》）

（如何比得上洗涤灵魂，修炼精神，依据道培育心志，依据德思考问题，即使行迹窘迫而道义通达，身体舒泰而事理皆通，这难道不很美好吗？）

Wouldn't it be far better to cleanse our souls, forge our character, nurture our aspiration or ponder any question under the guidance of Dao? That being the case, even if life remains tough, we will still feel morally accomplished. So long as we are in good health and understand things well, then everything is fine, isn't it? (*The History of Song of the Southern Dynasties*)

◎犹矿出金，如铅出银。超心炼冶，绝爱淄磷（lin）。空潭泻春，古镜照神。体素储洁，乘月返真。载瞻星辰，载歌幽人。流水今日，明月前身。（司空图《二十四诗品·洗炼》）

（像在矿石中炼出黄金，如从铅块里提取白银。专心反复冶炼，只为达于纯粹。如同清澈的春水直泻空潭，如同清晰的古镜映照物的神韵。体悟素朴真谛，蓄养纯洁天性，乘御皎洁月光，返归天宫仙境。瞻望天上星辰，吟唱幽居之士。清澈如同今日的春水，纯净就像明月的化身。）

This is like extracting gold from ores, or silver from chunks of lead. We smelt repeatedly for the sole purpose of attaining perfect purity. It is also like precious spring waters cascading down into an empty pool or a shining age-old mirror showing the charm of objects. We appreciate truth in all its simplicity, preserve our natural purity, and return to the celestial palace amid the beautiful moonlight. We look up at the sky full of stars, chanting in tribute to recluses of old. They are as precious as today's spring water and as pure as an incarnation of the bright moon. (Sikong Tu: Twenty-four Styles of Poetry)

◎不洗不净，不炼不纯。惟陈言之务去，独戛戛乎生新。（孙联奎《诗品臆说》）

（不淘洗就不纯净，不提炼就有杂质。只有坚决删除陈词滥调，才能生出独特的新意。）

Nothing will be clean until it is cleansed. Nothing will be pure until it is refined. Only by ridding ourselves of any banality, can we become truly original. (Sun Liankui: *A Random Interpretation of "Twenty-four Styles of Poetry"*)

乡饮酒礼

/xiāngyǐnjiǔlǐ/

Banquet for Community Leaders and Rural Elders

于乡间设酒宴酬宾之礼，是古代人伦生活中的一项重要礼仪。“乡”是古代的基层行政区划单位。“乡饮酒礼”在“乡”间举行，因其用意的不同，可大体分为两类：一类是宴请乡中德行贤良之士，以彰显对贤者的尊崇；另一类则由基层行政长官主持，宴请乡中年长之人，以表达对长者的尊敬与关爱。“乡饮酒礼”对于维护、调和基层的人伦秩序具有重要意义。

This was an important social function in ancient China. On the basis of their purpose, such banquets can generally be divided into two kinds: one was to entertain virtuous people in the locality in a display of respect for them; the other was hosted by local officials to entertain the elders to show respect and care for them. Such banquets were important in maintaining moral order in rural communities.

引例 Citation:

◎乡饮酒之礼，六十者坐，五十者立侍，以听政役，所以明尊长也。六十者三豆，七十者四豆，八十者五豆，九十者六豆，所以明养老也。（《礼记·乡饮酒义》）

（乡饮酒礼规定，六十岁以上的长者就座，五十岁以上的人站立陪侍，以听候政事差遣，所以彰显对年长者的尊敬。六十岁以上的长者享用三豆菜肴，七十岁以上者享用四豆菜肴，八十岁以上者享用五豆菜肴，九十岁以上者享用六豆菜肴，所以彰显对年长者的奉养。）

At banquets hosted for village elders, those who were over sixties sat, and those who were only in their fifties stood to serve them, and this shows that the elders were honored. Those in their sixties had three dishes, those in their seventies four, those in their eighties five and those in their nineties six, thus demonstrating care for the aged. (*The Book of Rites*)

絜矩之道

/xiéjǔzhīdào/

Principle for the Application of Rules and Norms

执掌法度的原则。出自《礼记·大学》。《大学》主张，为政者在执政、处事时应以“絜矩之道”对待他人。“絜”本指量物体粗细的绳子，“矩”是画方形或直角的曲尺，“絜矩”连用，意为所执持的规矩、法度。这里的规矩、法度即是要求为政者推己及人，以自身所好所恶体察他人的诉求，不以己所不欲强加于人，并以此作为政治、行事的法度。

This is a principle for the application of rules and norms, first cited in *The Great Learning*, a section of *The Book of Rites*. The book advocates the use of *xieju* by administrators in governance when dealing with people. *Xie* (絜) originally meant a string used for measuring the circumference of an object, while *ju* (矩) was a square used for drawing squares, rectangles or right angles. The combination of the two characters refers to rules and norms which must be upheld. In this case, the rules and norms require an administrator to put himself in others' position and judge their requests based on what he himself would want or not want, to not force upon others what he would reject, and to make this a norm in his governance and his work.

引例 Citation:

◎所恶（wù）于上，毋以使下；所恶于下，毋以事上；所恶于前，

毋以先后；所恶于后，毋以从前；所恶于右，毋以交于左；所恶于左，毋以交于右：此之谓絜矩之道。（《礼记·大学》）

（我所厌恶的上位者对待自己的言行，就不要用它来任使下属；我所厌恶的下属对待自己的言行，就不要用它来应对上位者；我所厌恶的前面之人的言行，就不要用它来对待后面的人；我所厌恶的后面之人的言行，就不要用它来对待前面的人；我所厌恶的右面之人的言行，就不要用它来对待左面的人；我所厌恶的左面之人的言行，就不要用它来对待右面的人：这就是所谓的"絜矩之道"。）

The words and deeds one abhors in a superior should not be applied to his subordinates; the words and deeds one abhors in a subordinate should not be applied to his superiors; the words and deeds one abhors in those who come before should not be applied to those who come after; the words and deeds one abhors in those who come after should not be applied to those who come before; the words and deeds one abhors in those on the right should not be applied to those on the left; the words and deeds one abhors in those on the left should not be applied to those on the right. This is what is known as the principle for the application of rules and norms. (*The Book of Rites*)

心术

／xīnshù／

The Art of the Mind

心的运作规则。最早见于《管子》《荀子》《礼记》等典籍。古人认为，心的作用的发挥遵循着一定的规则，这一规则即被称为“心术”。不过，各家对于“心术”具体内容的认识有所不同。“心术”或指心任使五官的原则，也指心与外物交接、认知外物的方式或态度。

This refers to the workings of the mind or heart, a term which first appeared in such classics as *Guanzi*, *Xunzi*, and *The Book of Rites*. In ancient times it was believed that a person's mind or heart played out its role in accordance with certain laws, which were referred to with this term. Nevertheless, different schools of thought had their own views on what it was about. The term also relates to how the human heart directs the movement of the five sensory organs, and with the way one communicates, and identifies oneself with the outside world.

引例 Citations:

◎“心之在体，君之位也；九窍之有职，官之分（fèn）也。”耳目者，视听之官也。心而无与于视听之事，则官得守其分矣。夫心有欲者，物过而目不见，声至而耳不闻也，故曰：“上离其道，下失其事。”故曰心术者，无为而制窍者也，故曰君。（《管子·心术上》）

（“心在人体之中，如同君主居于君位；九窍各有职守，如同百官各有其职。”耳目是主管视听的器官。心不干预视听之事，则耳目等器官可以各守其职。如果心有欲望，则事物从眼前经过却看不到，声音到达耳边却听不到，因此说：“居上位的人背离其原则，居下位的人就会荒废职事。”所以说心的运作规则，就是无为而控制九窍，所以称之为君。）

“The position of the mind or heart in the human body is similar to that of the king within a nation, and the nine orifices in the human body function in the same way as officials do at court.” Ears and eyes are for seeing and listening. When the mind does not intervene, the ears and eyes play their roles as they should. If however the mind is beset with desire, the eyes may fail to see what lies before them, and the ears may fail to hear what passes by. In the same way, “when those in superior positions act against the principles they are supposed to abide by, those in lower positions will hardly function as they are supposed to.” Therefore, doing nothing to hinder the operation of the nine human orifices is the art of the mind, which explains why it can be likened to a king. (*Guanzi*)

◎夫民有血气心知之性，而无哀乐喜怒之常，应感起物而动，然后心术形焉。（《礼记·乐记》）

（民众有血气、心知的本性，但哀乐喜怒情绪的表现却并不稳定，随着外物的刺激而感动，于是内心活动的路径就显现出来。）

People have aspirations and mental alert in their nature, but the emotions of sorrow, joy, happiness and anger are not manifested in a stable manner, and react to external stimulation. That is what gives away their inner thought. (*The Book of Rites*)

形名

/xíngmíng/

Form and Name

“形”指事物的形体，“名”指事物的名称。古人认为事物是有形的，有形之物具有自身的规定性，并与他者相区别。而“名”则用以指称这些有形之物。由“名”所构成的秩序，明确了有形之物彼此间的关系及其在整体秩序中的地位。有学派认为，事物固有的“形名”即已包含某种合理的秩序，为政者应遵循并维护这一“形名”秩序。也有学派认为，可以通过后天的刑罚、教化来塑造“形名”秩序。在强调刑罚所需的对事物、行事的分辨、判断时，“形名”又作“刑名”。

Xing (形) refers to the form of an object, and *ming* (名) refers to its name. The ancient Chinese believed that objects have forms, and that each formed object has its own specific nature which distinguishes it from other objects, whereas its name specifies the object. An order comprised of names establishes the relationships between the objects as well as their positions in the order. Certain schools of thought felt that the forms and names inherent in objects already incorporate a certain rational order, and that those who govern should abide by and uphold this order. Other schools of thought believed that an order of forms and names could be created after the fact through punishments (*xing*) and education. When emphasizing the need to analyze and judge things and actions while meting out punishments, 形名 (form and name) is also rendered as 刑名 (punishment and name).

引例 Citations:

◎故执道者之观于天下也，无执也，无处（chǔ）也，无为也，无私也。是故天下有事，无不自为刑（形）名声号矣。刑（形）名已立，声号已建，则无所逃迹匿正矣。（《黄帝四经·经法·道法》）

（因此持守道的君主对待天下，不固执，不居功，不妄为，不偏私。因此天下有事，无不自己确立事物的形名以及名号。形名已经确立，名号已经建立，那么各种事物都无所隐匿自己的形迹和常情了。）

Thus a ruler who follows moral principles will rule the realm without stubbornness, without claiming credit, without arrogance, and without biases. Hence in all matters, he will first determine the form and the name. Once form and name are ascertained, nothing will be able to conceal its traces or its normal state. (*The Four Classics of the Yellow Emperor*)

◎人主将欲禁奸，则审合刑名者，言与事也。（《韩非子·二柄》）

（君主想要禁止奸邪，则要审察核实事物的形名是否符合，也就是人们的言语和行事是否一致。）

If a ruler wishes to prohibit evil deeds, he must determine whether the forms and names of things accord with each other; that is, whether people's words accord with their deeds. (*Hanfeizi*)

杏林

/xìnglín/

Apricot Trees / Venerable Doctors with Good Skills

杏树林，对德行高尚、医术精湛的医生的美称，亦指代医学医药界。据东晋葛洪（281？—341）《神仙传》记载，三国时期名医董奉隐居庐山，无偿给人治病，只要求重症治愈者种杏五棵，轻症治愈者种杏一棵。几年后，他的住处就有了大片茂盛的杏树林。他用杏子换粮食，储存起来，用于救济贫苦人及其他需要帮助的人。后来，人们用“杏林”代指医德高尚、医术精湛的医生，近代一些医药团体和专业报刊也常以“杏林”取名，“杏林”遂成为医学医药界的代名词。它是“悬壶济世”理念的另一种表达形式。

This term refers to venerable doctors with good skills and by extension the entire profession of Chinese medicine. According to *Biographies of Deities and Immortals* by Ge Hong (281?–341), the famous doctor Dong Feng of the Three Kingdoms period lived on Mount Lu where he treated patients free of charge. All he asked from those who recovered from a serious illness was to plant five apricot trees and those who recovered from a minor ailment to plant one such tree. After some years, a lush wood of apricot trees appeared. He traded apricots for grain which he saved up to help the poor and needy. Later, people used apricot trees to refer to virtuous doctors with good skills, and in modern times, some medical organizations and journals in China used the designation “apricot trees" as their names. This term has become a synonym for Chinese medicine.

引例 Citation:

◎君异居山间，为人治病，不取钱物，使人重病愈者使栽杏五株，轻者一株。如此数年，计得十万余株，郁然成林。……买杏者皆于林中自平量之，不敢有欺者。君异以其所得粮谷赈救贫穷，供给行旅。（葛洪《神仙传》卷十）

（董奉住在山里，为人治病，不收钱财，只是让重病治愈者种杏五棵，轻者种杏一棵。这样几年下来，总共有十万余棵杏树，长成了茂盛的杏林。……买杏子的人都在林中自己称量，没人敢弄虚作假。董奉用换来的粮食救济穷人，还供往来旅客取用。）

Doctor Dong Feng who lived in a house on a mountain treated patients free of charge. He only asked his patients to plant apricot trees in exchange: five trees for patients of serious illness and one tree for patients of light illness. Several years later, 100,000 apricot trees were planted, forming lush woods... People came to buy apricots and weighed them by themselves, and no one cheated. Doctor Dong used the money to buy grains to give to the poor and travelers passing by. (Ge Hong: *Biographies of Deities and Immortals*)

悬壶济世

/xuánhú-jìshì/

Hang a Gourd (Practice Medicine) to Help the World

行医救助世人。“悬壶”即把装药的葫芦挂起来，作为行医卖药的招牌，泛指从事医疗职业；“济世”是对困苦之人提供救助。这一观念，使行医卖药超越了一般职业与谋生手段而被赋予了人文关怀的意义。它既是世人对于医者救死扶伤、治病救人行为的一种赞颂，也是医者用以自励的道德准则和价值判断。

This term means to help people by practicing medicine. “Hanging a gourd” refers to the tradition of using a gourd containing medications as a sign for those practicing and selling medicine; it is used more broadly to refer to those in the medical profession. “Helping the world” means providing aid and relief to those in distress. This concept elevates the practice of medicine above ordinary occupations and livelihoods, and imbues it with humanistic caring. It praises the deeds of physicians who care for the sick and dying, and is also a moral standard and value by which they should measure themselves.

引例 Citations:

◎市中有老翁卖药，悬一壶于肆头。(《后汉书·方术传下·费长房》)

（集市里面有一个卖药的老头儿，把一只药葫芦挂在集市的街头。）

There was an old man who sold medicine in the market. He hung a medicine gourd at his market stand. (*The History of the Later Han Dynasty*)

◎所以医人不得恃己所长，专心经略财物，但作救苦之心……志存救济，故亦曲碎论之，学者不可耻言之鄙俚也。（孙思邈《千金方·论大医精诚》）

（行医之人，不能仗着自己有一技之长，光想着谋取财物，而要怀有一颗把世人从苦痛中解救出来的善心……［我］志在救助世人，所以絮絮叨叨地讲论这些，希望学医的人不要耻笑我的想法很鄙陋。）

Someone who practices medicine must not simply rely on a particular skill and think only of acquiring money and goods. Rather, he must have a passion for relieving the sufferings of others… My aim is to help others, and I hope students of medicine will not mock my keeping saying so as being shallow. (Sun Simiao: *Essential Formulas for Emergencies*)

言者无罪，闻者足戒

/yánzhě-wúzuì, wénzhě-zújiè/

Those Who Speak Shouldn't Be Punished While Those Who Listen Should Take Warning.

无论意见是否正确，说的人没有罪责，而听的人足以获得警示。上到国家治理，下至组织、企业管理，执政者与管理者若要保障国家或组织、企业的良好运行，就必须充分了解下面的实际情况和群众意愿，调动各方面力量，发挥各方面作用。为此，必须造成一种健康和谐的人际环境，让人们畅所欲言，以便从各种言论中汲取有价值的意见。即便群众或下属所提意见不正确，领导者也不应责难，而要引以为戒。其中隐含有言论自由的思想和宽容精神。

Whether their opinions are correct or not, people who speak their minds should not be penalized and their messages should not be lost on their listeners. The term implies freedom of speech and a tolerant attitude towards criticism. To ensure proper governance and operation of a country, an organization, or a company, those in power and in management should have a good understanding of the situation on the ground as well as people's needs and wishes, so as to mobilize all the segments of the society to play their roles. The way to achieve such a result is to create healthy and harmonious relationships among people and let them speak their minds without fear so those in power can benefit from their various opinions and valuable insights. Even when the criticism from the general public or one's subordinates is not fully justified, those in leading positions should take warning rather than condemning the critics.

引例 Citations:

◎上以风化下，下以风刺上，主文而谲谏，言之者无罪，闻之者足以戒，故曰“风”。(《毛诗序》)

（执政者用风诗教化百姓，百姓也用风诗讥刺执政者，用富于文采的诗歌对执政者含蓄委婉地进行劝讽，歌咏的人不会因此获罪，听闻诗歌的人足以引起警诫，所以将这类诗称作“风”。）

Rulers use *feng* (ballads) to cultivate the people and the people use them to ridicule the rulers. So long as a critic advises the monarch mildly and through beautiful poetry, he will not be found guilty and the monarch he criticizes will become more careful in making decisions. These poems are called *feng*. (Introductions to *Mao's Version of The Book of Songs*)

◎言者无罪，闻者作戒。言者闻者，莫不两尽其心焉。(白居易《与元九书》)

（说的人没有罪责，听的人引以为戒。说者和听者双方都一心想着把事情做好。）

Those who speak their minds are not punished while those who listen should take warning. Both speakers and listeners only want to get things done in a satisfactory way. (Bai Juyi: Letter to Yuan Zhen)

言之无文，行而不远

/yán zhī wú wén, xíng ér bù yuǎn/

Lackluster Wording Never Travels Far.

语言如果缺乏文采和技巧，就不可能流传广泛久远。孔子（前551—前479）原话的意思是说，在外交场合，使臣须要擅长辞令，讲究语言技巧，才能达成目标、建立功业。进而引申出，一种思想如果想久远传播，就必须借助于有章法、有文采的书面文字。南朝刘勰（465？—520）在《文心雕龙》中征引了孔子的话，一方面充分肯定文辞的功效，另一方面是为了强调文章形式与技巧的重要性。该语阐明了语文对于明道经世的工具性作用，提升了文艺批评在思想文化史上的地位。

Lackluster writing or speech never travels far. What Confucius (551-479 BC) meant when he said this is that, in foreign relations, a diplomat should be eloquent and persuasive to achieve goals and become meritorious. Likewise, if an idea is to spread far or be remembered for long, it must be put to paper by rules of writing and with beautiful wording. In *The Literary Mind and the Carving of Dragons*, Liu Xie (465?-520) of the Southern Dynasties cited these words of Confucius to uphold the importance of diction and to stress the importance of an essay's layout and technique. This term highlights the instrumental role of writing in explaining and being useful to the world, thus raising the status of literary criticism in the history of thought and culture.

引例 Citations:

◎仲尼曰："志有之：'言以足志，文以足言。'不言，谁知其志？言之无文，行而不远。"（《左传·襄公二十五年》）

（孔子说："古书上记载：'言语用以表达意愿，文采和技巧是为了实现表达意愿的功能。'不说话，有谁能知道他的意愿？语言如果缺乏文采和技巧，就不可能流传广泛久远。"）

Confucius said: "According to ancient sources, 'Language is used to express wishes, and eloquence and literary skill perform an expressive function.' If he doesn't speak, who knows how he views anything? Even if he does, lackluster writing or speech will not travel far." (*Zuo's Commentaries on The Spring and Autumn Annals*)

◎言以文远，诚哉斯验。心术既形，英华乃赡。（《文心雕龙·情采》）

（语言要讲究文采和技巧才能流传广泛久远，这的确已经得到了证验。如果懂得了如何表现情志，就可以自如展现丰富的文采。）

Beautiful wording alone helps great ideas spread. This has been proved sufficiently true. Once we know how to express our feelings and aspirations, we will be able to display our literary talent with ease. (Liu Xie: *The Literary Mind and the Carving of Dragons*)

一阐提

/yīchǎntí/

Icchantika

字面意思为“有欲求的人”，指因为缺乏引生善果的根本条件，而无法成就觉悟、实现解脱的人。又称“断善根者”。关于一阐提的义理争论，主要集中在众生能否成佛的问题上。如唯识法相一系，就一阐提缺乏善因而言，主张必不得成就；如来藏、华严等系则认为一切众生皆有佛性，且待开显而已。前者将一阐提作为本性，后者似以其为暂时的状态。

Icchantika literally means one who desires. It refers to a person who is destitute of good conditions that lead to favorable results, such as awakening and liberation. Hence, it is also glossed as one deprived of merits. The major doctrinal debate over this concept is whether all sentient beings, including *icchantikas*, are capable of achieving the Buddhahood. In the view of the *Vijñaptimātra* School (alias the Mind-only School), for example, *icchantikas* are devoid of proper conditions in nature, therefore would never achieve the final goal. Whereas, in *Tathāgatagarbha* and *Avataṃsaka* traditions, all sentient beings are born with the nature of a Buddha, which only anticipates to manifest (at some point). Generally speaking, the former standpoint takes *icchantika* as innate, while the latter understands it as a temporary status.

引例 Citations:

◎我常宣说一切众生悉有佛性，乃至一阐提等亦有佛性。一阐提等无有善法，佛性亦善，以未来有故，一阐提等悉有佛性。（《大般涅槃经·师子吼菩萨品》）

（我一直宣说，一切众生都有成佛的可能性，即使是断除了一切善根的人也有佛性。断除善根的人虽然没有善业积累，但其本有的佛性是好的。由于未来仍可能积行善业，所以说这些人也都有佛性。）

I have often proclaimed the universality of the Buddha-nature in all sentient beings, including *icchantikas* (literally one who is subject to great desire, hence according to certain schools should be bereft of all the possibilities to achieve Buddhahood). *Icchantikas*, though devoid of any meritorious deeds accumulated so far throughout their past lives, still possess the Buddha-nature and thus will be able to engage in the wholesome activities in the future. (*Sutra of the Great Nirvana*)

◎合经及论，"阐提"有三……一因成果不成，谓大悲阐提；二果成因不成，谓有性断善阐提；三因果俱不成，谓无性阐提，二乘定性。（释窥基《成唯识论掌中枢要》卷上（本））

（结合经论所说，一阐提可分为三类……其一，是具备条件，但未实现成佛结果的，这叫大悲阐提；其二，是不具备条件，但能够借助佛力成就结果的，这叫有佛性而断除善根的阐提；其三，是条件和结果都不存在，叫做无性阐提，即只有实现声闻、缘觉两种道路的本性。）

Taking scriptures and commentaries into consideration, there are three types of *icchantikas*... The first type refers to *icchantikas* out of compassion who are ready with the conditions to emancipate but do not realize it since they vowed to liberate all beings before they realize the nirvana. The second type refers to *icchantikas* endowed with the Buddha-nature but without proper deeds to realize the Buddhahood, who could expect the result facilitated by the power of a Buddha while lack of sufficient conditions. The third type refers to *icchantikas* deprived of the Buddha-nature, who have neither the conditions nor the result-to-be and are destined to follow the two inferior paths of *śrāvaka* and *pratyekabuddha*. (Shi Kuiji: *A Commentary on Collected Commentaries to the Perfection of Consciousness-only*)

医者仁心

/yīzhě-rénxīn/

The Caring Heart of a Physician

医者要有仁爱之心。其基本精神，古已有之。唐朝著名医学家孙思邈（581—682）在《千金方·论大医精诚》中，已经有医者应存有恻隐之心也即“仁心”的相关论述。它要求医者对患者要有大爱之心、悲悯之情、救苦之志，不计个人得失，一心治病救人，而医者也因此成为“苍生大医”（众生景仰的伟大医者）。此语可谓中华医学人文精神的典型表达。

A physician must have a caring heart. This essential spirit has existed since ancient times. In the chapter “On the Skill and Sincerity of a Master Physician” of his work *Essential Formulas for Emergencies*, the famous Tang Dynasty physician Sun Simiao (581-682) discussed how a physician should have a compassionate heart, that is, a caring heart. A physician is expected to have great love, a sense of empathy and a desire to relieve suffering; he must disregard personal interests and focus entirely on treating the sick. In so doing, the physician becomes a “master physician to all the people,” a great physician held in high esteem by all the people. This expression can be considered a classic expression of the humanist spirit of Chinese medicine.

引例 Citations:

◎凡大医治病，必当安神定志，无欲无求，先发大慈恻隐之心，誓愿普救含灵之苦。（孙思邈《千金方·论大医精诚》）

（凡是杰出的医生给人治病，一定会安定心神，无欲无求，对病人先有慈悲同情之心，有愿意广泛救助世人脱离苦痛的决心。）

When a master physician treats an illness, he must be calm in spirit, and free from desires; he must first have a compassionate heart, and be committed to relieving the sufferings of all people. (Sun Simiao: *Essential Formulas for Emergencies*)

◎医乃仁术也，笔之于书，欲天下同归于仁也。（汪机《〈推求师意〉序》）

（治病是充满仁爱之心的道术，作者写这本书，是希望全天下的医者都同样怀有一颗仁爱之心。）

The practice of medicine is one which is filled with caring. The author has written this book in the hope that all physicians will likewise have caring hearts. (Wang Ji: Preface to *A Study of Our Teacher's Medical Thinking*)

◎故医者能正其心术，虽学不足，犹不至于害人。（徐大椿《医学源流论·医家论》）

（所以医生如果能够端正自己的心术，即便医术不高，还不至于危害病人。）

Thus if a physician has the correct mindset, even if his skills are imperfect, he will at least not harm his patients. (Xu Dachun: *The Origin and Development of Illnesses*)

意不称物，文不逮意

/yì bù chèn wù, wén bù dài yì/

Ideas Cannot Match Actual Things and Words Cannot Fully Express Ideas.

人的心意或文章的构意不能完全反映事物的情状，而文章的语言或文辞又无法完全表达内心的想法。这是西晋陆机（261—303）《文赋》中对创作心理的描述和分析，具体所指是：由外物激发的意念或创作想法丰富而不明确，作者难以完全把握由外物所激发的全部心意，所捕捉到的可能只是其中一部分；而语言又难以将它们完全表达出来，更不可能穷尽由外物激发或与外物关联的全部意蕴。在认识及实践领域，主体对外物产生明确的认识或意愿，语言能够比较明确地记录认识并表达意愿，而文学创作则常常存在词不达意、言不尽意的难题。这也表明文学阐释较之学术经典解释具有更大的空间。陆机揭示了文学创作与接受的特征，推动了文学自觉。

This happens when inner thoughts or a written text's general idea cannot fully reflect the actual state of things, and when diction cannot fully express inner thoughts. It is a description and analysis of the psychology of writing by Lu Ji (261-303) of the Western Jin Dynasty in his literary theoretic work, "The Art of Writing." Specifically, inner thoughts or creative ideas triggered by external things can be diverse yet ambiguous and the author grasps only some of these. Language, too, has difficulty in expressing them fully, not to mention all the implications triggered by or related to external things. In the domain of everyday human cognition and practice, language can, by and large, clearly record the subject's thoughts and express his wishes with regard to external things. But in literary creation, words often fail to do so. This also explains why literary interpretation enjoys greater latitude than purely academic interpretation. Lu Ji revealed this essential characteristic of literary creation and reception, thus promoting the development of literature under its own standards.

引例 Citation:

◎恒患意不称物，文不逮意，盖非知之难，能之难也。（陆机《文赋》）

（自己经常苦于人的心意或文章构意不能完全反映事物的情状，而语言或文章的文辞又无法完全表达内心的想法。大概这个问题，认识它并不难，解决它却很难。）

Inner thoughts or an article's general idea cannot fully reflect the actual state of things, and diction cannot fully express inner thoughts – a predicament I often find myself in. It is far easier to recognize this problem than solve it. (Lu Ji: The Art of Writing)

因材施教

／yīncái-shījiào／

Audience-based Education

根据人的资质、志趣等实施教育、教学。“材”指人的资质、志趣、受教育程度等因素。这是孔子（前551—前479）最早实践、经后人总结概括而确立的教育、教学原则。《礼记·中庸》所说的“率性”（遵循人的天性）、《周易》所说的“尽性”（充分发挥天性），可以说是这一原则的基础理念，它至今仍被广为提倡，其要旨是：教育、教学在内容选择、方法运用、目标设定等方面，要适应受教育者的个体差异，以期达到更好效果。这一原则得到心理学、教育学的论证，已经成为现代教育科学的基本理念。

This term means to educate and teach according to people's caliber and their interests. *Cai* (材) refers to factors such as people's caliber and interests, and their level of education. This is an educational and pedagogical principle first practiced by Confucius (551-479 BC), and later summarized and established by others. We may say that the core concepts of this principle are *shuaixing* (率性 acting in accordance with human nature) as described in *The Book of Rites*, and *jinxing* (尽性 making full use of human nature) as described in *The Book of Changes*. It has been widely accepted to this day, and its gist is that in education and pedagogy, the choice of subject matter, methods and goals must vary according to the individual characteristics of the audience if they are to achieve better outcomes. This principle has been corroborated through psychology and pedagogy, and has become a fundamental concept in the modern science of education.

引例 Citations:

◎子曰："中人以上，可以语上也；中人以下，不可以语上也。"（《论语·雍也》）

（孔子说："对资质中等以上的人，可以讲高深的道理；对资质中等以下的人，不可以讲高深的道理。"）

Confucius said, "You can discuss profound issues with someone who is above average; you cannot discuss profound issues with someone who is below average." (*The Analects*)

◎天之生物，必因其材而笃焉。（《礼记·中庸》）

（上天生养万物，必定根据它们的资质天性而厚待它们。）

Heaven gave birth to all living things, and it must treat them according to their characteristics. (*The Book of Rites*)

◎因材施教，士多因以得名，时有朱门弟子之目。（《清史稿·朱筠传》）

（[朱筠]因材施教，很多读书人经过他的培养而成名，当时有“朱门弟子”之称。）

Because Zhu Jun adjusted his teaching to his audience, many scholars who studied with him achieved fame, and they were known at the time as "pupils of Zhu." (*Draft History of the Qing Dynasty*)

因革

/yīngé/

Inheritance and Innovation

既有所继承又有所创革。“因”是继承、沿袭，“革”是革新、改变。这一思想可溯源到孔子（前551—前479）。在孔子看来，夏商周三代礼制都是在前代基础上根据当时的历史条件有所损益的。所谓“损益”就蕴含了因革的观念。汉代扬雄（前53—公元18）对“因革”作了比较系统的阐发。这一思想后来被南朝刘勰（465？—520）用于文论，进而衍生出“通变”概念。“因革”“通变”体现的都是继承与创新的对立统一，强调基于历史与传统的变化，在继承前人经验、成果的基础上进行创新，既不是泥古不化，也不是追新逐异。不仅是文艺创作，其他如学术发展乃至国家治理，皆同此理。

This term highlights the relationship between inheritance and innovation. *Yin* (因) implies inheritance or adoption, whereas *ge* (革) means reform or innovation. The whole notion can be traced back to Confucius (551-479 BC). In his view, the Xia, Shang and Zhou dynasties had all modified their respective codes of etiquette in accordance with their own circumstances and on the basis of a previous era's established rules. "Modified" here implies the idea of innovation grounded in inheritance. Yang Xiong (53 BC-AD 18) of the Han Dynasty expounded this idea more systematically. This concept was later used by Liu Xie (465?-520) of the Southern Dynasties in literary criticism, giving rise to the notion of "continuity and change." All these ideas reflect a unity of opposites, stressing constant change in history and tradition, favoring innovation grounded in past experience and achievements, as well as avoiding either unquestioning adherence to convention or blind pursuit of novelty. Besides literary and artistic creation, the concept above is also applicable to academic research and even the governance of a country.

引例 Citations:

◎子曰："殷因于夏礼，所损益，可知也；周因于殷礼，所损益，可知也。其或继周者，虽百世可知也。"（《论语·为政》）

（孔子说："殷商沿袭夏朝的礼仪制度，所废除或所增加的，是可以知道的；周朝沿袭殷商的礼仪制度，所废除或所增加的，也是可以知道的。那么，假定有继承周朝而当政的人，就是以后一百代，也是可以预先知道的。"）

Confucius said: "The Shang Dynasty inherited the Xia Dynasty's codes of etiquette with abridgements and additions, which can be known. The Zhou Dynasty followed the Shang's codes of etiquette with abridgements and additions, which can also be known. Therefore, if there should be a successor to the Zhou Dynasty, even a hundred generations from now, its codes of etiquette could be foretold." (*The Analects*)

◎夫道有因有循，有革有化。因而循之，与道神之；革而化之，与时宜之。故因而能革，天道乃得；革而能因，天道乃驯。……故知因而不知革，物失其则；知革而不知因，物失其均。（扬雄《太玄·玄莹》）

（道的运行法则既有继承又有变革。只有懂得继承，才能穷尽道的神奇；只有懂得变革，才能与当世合宜。所以懂得有继承又有变革，才能领悟道的运行法则；懂得有变革又有继承，道的运行法则才能为人所用。……所以只懂得继承不懂得变革，就不能深刻把握万物的普遍法则；只懂得变革不懂得继承，就不能深刻把握万物之间的平衡规律。）

The operation of Dao involves inheritance and continuity, and innovation and change. Only through inheritance and continuity can we fully explore the mystery of Dao. Only through innovation and change can we meet the needs of our times. Thus, respecting tradition while pursuing innovation helps us understand the laws of Dao, and pursuing innovation while respecting tradition helps us apply the laws of Dao... Therefore, if we overemphasize tradition to the neglect of innovation, we will fail to fully understand universal laws; if we focus on innovation at the expense of tradition, we will fail to master the rules of equilibrium. (Yang Xiong: *Supreme Mystery*)

◎古来辞人，异代接武，莫不参（sān）伍以相变，因革以为功。物色尽而情有余者，晓会通也。（刘勰《文心雕龙·物色》）

（自古以来的文人作家，历代前后相继，无不靠着错综变化、有继承又有革新而收到成效。景物有穷尽而情思写不尽，就是因为他们懂得融会和变通。）

Ever since ancient times, writers from generation to generation have made remarkable achievements, through inheritance, change, and innovation, in accordance with circumstances. Scenes have limits, but human feelings linger on due to our ability to integrate and accommodate. (Liu Xie: *The Literary Mind and the Carving of Dragons*)

隐士

／yǐnshì／

Hermit / Recluse

有能力为官或为君却选择隐居避世之人。在古代社会中，“隐士”做出隐居的选择有着不同的原因：其一，厌倦日常生活中繁文缛节的虚伪、浮华，而追求质朴、自然的生活。其二，不满于现实政治的昏乱，或不愿同流合污，或为避免迫害，而选择隐居避世。其三，甘愿更贤能之人取代自己为官、为君，而主动避让退隐。“隐士”往往具有高洁的品质，但并非社会的主流。刻意或过度追求隐逸的生活，反而会失于虚伪，或造成社会责任的缺失。

In ancient China, this term referred to those who were capable of being an official or even a ruler but who chose to live in seclusion. They had different reasons for this. One might be that they were tired of formalities and red tape and considered such a role as hypocritical, and wished instead for a simple and natural way of life. Another reason was that some were dissatisfied with the corrupt politics of the day, and did not want to get involved, or wished to avoid being persecuted. Yet others chose to withdraw into a hermit-like way of life just because they wanted to give away their posts or positions to those who were more capable and more virtuous. Such people usually had good virtue, but they were not mainstream. It might however be considered being hypocritical to persist in such a way of life for its own sake, and be seen as dereliction of social responsibility.

引例 Citations:

◎子路从而后，遇丈人，以杖荷蓧（diào）。子路问曰："子见夫子乎？"丈人曰："四体不勤，五谷不分，孰为夫子？"植其杖而芸。子路拱而立。止子路宿，杀鸡为黍而食（sì）之，见（xiàn）其二子焉。明日，子路行，以告。子曰："隐者也。"使子路反见之。至，则行矣。子路曰："不仕无义。长幼之节，不可废也；君臣之义，如之何其废之？欲洁其身，而乱大伦。君子之仕也，行其义也。道之不行，已知之矣。"（《论语·微子》）

（子路跟随孔子而落在后面，遇到一位老人，用手杖挑着除草的工具。子路问道："您看到我的老师了吗？"老人回答："不劳苦四肢，不能辨别五谷，谁是你的老师呢？"将手杖插在一边去除草了。子路拱手而恭敬地站着。老人留子路住宿，杀鸡做饭给子路吃，又叫他两个儿子出来相见。第二天，子路离开，赶上孔子后报告了此事。孔子说："这是位隐士。"让子路回去再拜见他。子路到了那里，老人已经离开了。子路说："不出仕为官是不合道义的。长幼之间的礼节，尚且不可以废除；君臣之间的职分，怎么能废除呢？想要不玷污自身，却悖乱了人伦。君子出仕为官，是行其应尽的道义。正道不能推行，早已知道了。”）

Accompanying his teacher Confucius on a trip, Zilu had fallen behind. When he ran into an old man carrying a weed basket on the staff upon his back, Zilu asked: "Did you see my teacher?" The old man answered: "You can neither toil with your limbs nor tell apart the different grains. Who is your teacher?" So saying, the old man put his stick aside and set about cutting wild grass. Zilu stood there in reverence. The old man then asked Zilu to stay the night, made a chicken dish for dinner, and asked his two sons to meet Zilu. Zilu left the following day and told Confucius about this encounter when he caught up with his teacher. Confucius said: "He is a hermit." He urged Zilu to go back and pay his respects. Yet, the old man had left when he got there. Zilu thereupon said: "It is against morality and justice to refuse the duties of an official. If etiquette between adults and children are not to be neglected, how can the responsibilities and obligations between a monarch and court officials be ignored? In seeking to maintain his purity, he has allowed human relations to fall into confusion. It is to observe morality and justice for a scholar to assume official duties. The righteous way cannot be followed through. This is rather obvious." (*The Analects*)

◎古之所谓隐士者，非伏其身而弗见（xiàn）也，非闭其言而不出也，非藏其知（zhì）而不发也，时命大谬也。（《庄子·缮性》）

（古时所谓的隐士，并不是藏匿自己的行迹而不被人看到，并不是闭塞自己的言论而不说话，并不是隐藏自己的智慧而不施用，是因为时势大相悖谬的缘故。）

For ancient hermits, it is not that they meant to hide their whereabouts, to shut up about their own opinions or to withhold their wisdom from application. It is rather that the condition of the times was against them. (*Zhuangzi*)

◎或隐居以求其志，或回避以全其道，或静己以镇其躁，或去危以图其安，或垢俗以动其概，或疵物以激其清。然观其甘心畎（quǎn）亩之中，憔悴江海之上，岂必亲鱼鸟乐林草哉，亦云性分（fèn）所至而已。（《后汉书·逸民传序》）

（有的人通过隐居以达成自己的志向，有的人通过回避世事以保全自己的道德，有的人通过安静心性以克制自己的急躁，有的人避开危险以希求平安，有的人视世俗为污垢而振奋节操，有的人因看不惯世事而激励洁行。然而看他们甘心在田野中生活，在江海上落拓憔悴，难道一定是为了亲近鱼鸟、喜爱山林草木吗？也可说是他们的天性使其如此而已。）

Some lead a secluded life in order to fulfill their aspirations, some stay away from worldly affairs in order to keep intact their morals, some enjoy a peaceful life just to contain their own hot temper, some shun danger to keep themselves safe, some consider worldly life as contaminated just to keep their moral integrity, and some just cannot accept the worldly life to seek a simpler and cleaner life. However, when seeing them reconciling themselves to working in open fields and looking unconventional and haggard, we cannot but wonder whether they really love to stay with birds and fish and are really fond of forest and grasses. It may be their own innate characters that have led them to such a way of life. (*The History of the Later Han Dynasty*)

隐显

/yǐnxiǎn/

Concealment and Revelation

“隐”指隐讳含藏，“显”指鲜明显扬。作为文艺术语，它们指诗文创作过程中，有些事理须要隐讳含藏，有些事理须要鲜明显扬，体现在语义和文辞上，则或含蓄或显豁，理想的艺术境界是隐显有度。文辞含蓄，语义隐讳，并不是晦涩难懂，而是耐人寻味；文辞明白，语义显豁，也不是直白外露，而是明确清楚。从普遍意义来讲，“隐”与“显”并不是非此即彼的对立关系，而是可以互相转变流动的辩证关系，其间体现“道”的变化。

“Concealment” refers to keeping things hidden, whereas “revelation” means making things abundantly clear. As an artistic and literary term, this pair of opposites refers to a creative process in which some things need to be hidden and others abundantly clear. When applied to semantics or rhetoric, it refers to subtle or explicit modes of expression. An ideal work of art is marked by a proper balance between concealment and revelation. Understatement or hidden meaning does not mean being cryptic, but rather being profound in significance. On the other hand, plainness of wording or conspicuousness of meaning does not mean sheer transparency, but rather clarity. Generally speaking, concealment and revelation are not mutually exclusive. They are instead interchangeable and feature two-way dialectic mobility, revealing Dao in constant change.

引例 Citations:

◎四象精义以曲隐，五例微辞以婉晦，此隐义以藏用也。故知繁略殊形，隐显异术，抑引随时，变通适会，征之周孔，则文有师矣。（刘勰《文心雕龙·征圣》）

（《周易》中的四种卦象，其道理精深而曲折隐晦，《春秋》中的五种记事条例，其文辞细微而婉转含蓄，这是用含蓄隐微的意义来暗含文章作用的例子。因此可知繁和简有不同的面貌，隐与显有不同的表达方法，或压缩或加以发挥要根据当时的要求，写作上的变化要适应不同的情况，用周公、孔子的言论来检验，那么写文章就有了师法了。）

In *The Book of Changes*, there is mention of four divinatory symbols which are of profound and intricate meanings. Recorded in *The Spring and Autumn Annals* are five essential requirements of writing, which are themselves artful and subtle. Both of these examples illustrate the function of a piece of writing by resorting to the subtle nuances of meaning. Thus, it can be seen that simplicity and complexity have different outward features, and concealment and revelation have different modes of expression. Authors should curtail or expand the contents of their writing depending on circumstances, adapting to a variety of situations. Good writing is achievable by testing it against the teachings of the Duke of Zhou and Confucius. (Liu Xie: *The Literary Mind and the Carving of Dragons*)

◎窃惟《中庸》一篇，圣贤之渊源也，体用隐显，成己成物备矣。（张栻（shì）《跋〈中庸集解〉》）

（我个人认为《中庸》这一篇文章，是圣贤思想的本源，它的本体、作用或含蓄或显扬，成就自己、成就外物的方法都齐备了。）

I personally believe that the essay titled "The Doctrine of the Mean" is the source of sagely thought. It conceals or reveals its essence and functions in accord with circumstances, resulting in accomplishment for self and other. (Zhang Shi: Postscript to *Collected Explanations of and Commentaries on The Doctrine of the Mean*)

有病不治，常得中医

/yǒu bìng bù zhì, cháng dé zhōng yī/

Self-treating an Illness Can Usually Get a Good Result.

有病不去就医，其结果如同请中等水平的医生诊治一样（与“久病成医”意思相近）。“不治”，不请大夫，不去医治；“得”，相当，能够；“中医”，中等水平的医生或疗效，有时作“合乎医理”解（“中”读 zhòng）。这是《汉书·艺文志》记载的谚语，后来演变为“不服药胜中医”等说法。其本意是说，与其请来庸医治病，胡乱施治，非但没能将病治好，反而使病情更糟，还不如不请医生；况且有些疾病即使不治，也能自愈。此语表达了人们对庸医的拒斥和对良医的期盼，也隐含这样的观念：某些疾病可以自愈，无须施治。

The proverb, which is similar in meaning with the concept “prolonged suffering from an illness will turn a person into a doctor,” comes from *The History of the Han Dynasty*. It later changed into sayings like “taking no medicine is better than seeing a mediocre doctor,” which means essentially it is better not to see a doctor than to be mistreated by a mediocre doctor. Incompetent treatment will make a patient sicker rather than better. On the other hand, certain illnesses can recover automatically over time without treatment. This saying speaks to the rejection of people of mediocre doctors and longing for competent ones. At the same time, it also implies the notion that some diseases can cure themselves over time without treatment.

引例 Citations:

◎［经方］及失其宜者，以热益热，以寒增寒，精气内伤，不见（xiàn）于外，是所独失也。故谚曰："有病不治，常得中医。"（《汉书·艺文志》）

（及至有些药方不适合病情，用热性药物使人更热、用寒性药物使人更寒，对人的精气神造成伤害，而身体表面并不显现，这完全是用药不当造成的失误。所以谚语说："有病不去就医，其结果如同请中等水平的医生诊治一样。"）

And some prescriptions are not appropriate to treat diseases. Medicines that are hot in nature make patients even hotter whereas those that are cold in nature make patients even colder. They damage their essence, energy, and spirit, though it does not show any symptoms in appearance. That is the mistake solely of misusing medicines. Hence the proverb: self-treating one's illness can usually get a good result. (*The History of the Han Dynasty*)

◎世言"不服药胜中医"，此语虽不可通行，然疾无甚苦，与其为庸医妄投药反败之，不得为无益也。（叶梦得《避暑录话》卷下）

（世人说"有病不吃药，胜过中等水平的医生"，这话虽然不适用于所有病情，但若是病得不很严重，与其被医术平庸的大夫胡乱开药让病情变得更糟，还不如这样做更好。）

People say, "Self-treating one's illness can usually get a good result." That saying may not apply to all diseases, but if one's illness is not serious, practicing self-treatment may be better than trusting a mediocre doctor who may prescribe wrong medicines and make one's condition even worse. (Ye Mengde: *Essays Written on Summer Holidays*)

◎古谚有"不服药为中（zhòng）医"之说，自宋以前已有之。盖因医道失传，治人多误，病者又不能辨医之高下，故不服药。虽不能愈病，亦不至为药所杀。况病苟非死症，外感渐退，内伤渐复，亦能自愈，故云"中医"。（徐大椿《医学源流论·轻药愈病论》）

（古代谚语有"有病不吃药，亦合乎医理"的说法，这话在宋朝以前就有了。这大概是因为医术失传了，医生给人治病经常失误，而患者又不能辨别医生水平的高低，所以干脆不吃药。病虽然好不了，但也不至于被庸医所开的药害死。况且，如果不是致死的病症，体表的病症逐渐消退，体内的伤病逐渐平复，也能自愈，所以说"合乎医理"。）

An ancient proverb goes, "self-treating one's illness makes medical sense, too." That proverb was perhaps already prevalent before the Song Dynasty. The reason may be due to the loss of the past medical skills, resulting in frequent occurrence of wrong diagnosis and treatment. Frustrated and yet unable to judge the skills of the doctors, patients simply stop taking medicines. That may carry the danger of never recovering from their illness but may save them from being murdered by quacks. Moreover, if the illness is not life-threatening, it will gradually cure itself. Therefore, such an approach "makes medical sense." (Xu Dachun: *The Origin and Development of Illnesses*)

元和体

／Yuánhé tǐ／

The Yuanhe Style of Poetry

指唐宪宗元和年间（806—820）开始流行的诗歌体式及风格。有广狭二义：广义的理解指元和以来的各种新体诗文，一般认为元和以后流行的新的文风、诗风，是由韩愈（768—824）、元稹（779—831）、白居易（772—846）、张籍（767？—830？）等元和年间的著名作家开创的；狭义的理解则是指元稹、白居易诗歌中的长篇排律和中短篇杂体诗。元稹、白居易的诗歌注重叙事，如《连昌宫词》《长恨歌》《琵琶行》都是长篇叙事诗的代表作；其次是注重诗歌形式的通俗化，具体说就是诗的语言明白晓畅，容易为读者理解记忆；注意诗歌与音乐的结合，韵律的优美和谐，便于唱诵。

This term refers to the poetic style most popular during the rule of Emperor Xianzong (806-820) of the Tang Dynasty under the reign title of Yuanhe. It can be understood either broadly or narrowly. In a broad sense, the Yuanhe style of poetry refers to all new forms of verse prevalent from the Yuanhe era onward, created by famed Yuanhe-era writers such as Han Yu (768-824), Yuan Zhen (779-831), Bai Juyi (772-846), and Zhang Ji (767?-830?). In a narrow sense, it refers to lengthy regulated verse and shorter poems of mixed metrical schemes in poetic composition of the works of Yuan Zhen and Bai Juyi. Both poets paid careful attention to the narrative function of poetry. For example, "A Song of the Lianchang Palace," "A Song of Unending Sorrow," and "A Song of the Pipa Player" are all representative of lengthy narrative poetry. They also pursued a more popular style of poetry, using vernacular language which was intelligible and easy to remember for ordinary readers. Moreover, they tried to combine poetry and music, making their works rhythmically beautiful and harmonious, thus suitable for chanting or singing.

引例 Citations:

◎元和已后，为文笔则学奇诡于韩愈，学苦涩于樊宗师；歌行则学流荡于张籍；诗草则学矫激于孟郊，学浅切于白居易，学淫靡于元稹，俱名为“元和体”。（李肇《唐国史补》卷下）

（元和以后，写文章的人学韩愈的奇特怪异，学樊宗师的晦涩生僻；写歌行体长诗的人则学张籍的放荡不羁；写诗的人则学孟郊的奇异偏激，学白居易的浅易切当，学元稹的浮华艳丽，这些当时都称为“元和体”。）

Since the Yuanhe era, essay writers have come to imitate Han Yu's oddity and Fan Zongshi's opaqueness; writers of long poetic songs have taken fancy to Zhang Ji's bold, uninhibited ways; and poets embraced Meng Jiao's strangeness and extremity, Bai Juyi's intelligibility and aptness, and Yuan Zhen's pomposity and flamboyance. All this constitutes what is known as the "Yuanhe style." (Li Zhao: *A Supplement to Liu Su's Dynastic History*)

◎［元］稹聪警绝人，年少有才名，与太原白居易友善，工为诗，善状咏风态物色，当时言诗者称元白焉。自衣冠士子，至闾阎下俚，悉传讽之，号为"元和体"。(《旧唐书·元稹传》)

（元稹聪慧过人，年少时就有才名，与太原人白居易是好友，他们都擅长写诗，善于描摹歌咏事物的形态景色，当时谈论诗歌的人都会提及元白。从士大夫、儒林学子到市井百姓，都在流传歌咏他们的诗，称之为"元和体"。）

Yuan Zhen was unusually talented and achieved renown at a very young age. He and Bai Juyi, a native of Taiyuan were good friends. Both of them were remarkable at writing poetry, depicting and extolling things in all colors and forms. All lovers of poetry at the time would mention Yuan Zhen and Bai Juyi together. Everybody, whether they were scholar-officials, students or ordinary people, was found chanting their poetry, calling it "Yuanhe-style poetry." (*The Old Tang History*)

圆融

／yuánróng／

Consummate Interfusion

圆满融通。在佛教典籍中，圆融既指各种事物之间相互融通统摄的本来状态，也指避免偏执任一见地的真理观。如天台（tāi）宗说空、假、中三谛，分疏三个层面的真理，有别于传统的二谛，凸显了不落空有两边、又不离两边的圆融意旨。而华严的“六相圆融”，指出一切事物都有总、别、同、异、成、坏三对看似矛盾的方面，其实超越了概念的对立，可于一体具现。

In Buddhist scriptures, “consummate interfusion” has two meanings: (1) the original state of all things, which are interfused with and governed by each other, and (2) a viewpoint on truth that argues against adherence to any judgment. The Tiantai School interprets “consummate interfusion” in this way: it develops the concept of *satyadvaya* (the two truths) into “the three levels of truth” – the empty truth, the false truth, and the middle-way truth. According to this theory, one shall neither descend into nor detach oneself from the two extremes: emptiness and existence. Such non-duality demonstrates the nature of consummate interfusion. The Huayan School offers another interpretation with “the consummate interfusion of six aspects.” It argues that all things can be judged from six aspects: the general, the particular, the identity, the differentiated, the integrated, and the destructive aspect. Although they appear as three opposites, these aspects, consubstantial with one another, transcend conceptual opposition.

引例 Citation:

◎分别者，但法有粗妙：若隔历三谛，粗法也；圆融三谛，妙法也。（释智颢（yǐ）《妙法莲华经玄义》卷一上）

（所谓差别，只是说认识的粗浅和精妙之分：如果三谛之间互相排斥，这就是一种粗浅的认识；如果三谛互相融通统摄，则为精妙的认识。）

The distinction lies in the subtlety of dharma. The superficial dharma deals with the three truths separately, while the subtle one perfectly interfuses them. (Shi Zhiyi: *Profound Meaning of The Lotus Sutra of the Wonderful Dharma*)

至乐无乐

/zhìlè-wúlè/

Utmost Happiness Lies in Not Aware of the Happiness.

至高的快乐是内心祥和而超越乐与不乐的判断。庄子（前369？—前286）认为，快乐应该依从于自己的本心，如果以世俗观念为判断依据，可能会背离生命的本质；如果为情感和欲望所驱使，可能会伴随失落与伤害。快乐与否的判断实际上源于对利害得失的判断，而利害得失是相对的、可变的，因此，忘却得失利害、没有了快乐意念才是"至乐"的境界。"至乐无乐"说体现出中国古代文人学士通达的心性、自由多元的人生价值观，激发了他们反思、批判与超越的精神。

Utmost happiness is an inner peace that transcends any judgment as to whether we are happy or not. Zhuangzi (369?-286 BC) held that happiness should be dictated solely by the heart. If we measure happiness against a worldly criterion, we may lose sight of life's essential purpose. If we are driven by emotions and base desires, harm and loss may be the result. Our happiness in fact depends on our judgment of loss or gain. However, loss or gain is relative and subject to change. Only when we totally forget this question can we attain utmost happiness. This term reflects the spiritual magnanimity and the open, pluralistic worldview of ancient Chinese scholars, while urging them to greater effort at self-reflection, criticism, and transcendence.

引例 Citations:

◎果有乐无有哉？ 吾以无为诚乐矣，又俗之所大苦也。故曰："至乐无乐，至誉无誉。"（《庄子·至乐》）

（世间果真是存在快乐呢，还是不存在呢？我认为没有快乐与不快乐的意识才是真正的快乐，而这又是世人为之大感苦恼的事情。所以说："至高的快乐是无需感到快乐，最高的荣誉是无需众人赞誉。"）

Is there happiness or not in this world of ours? My belief is that utmost happiness lies in not even being aware of it. However, this very thought is exactly what agonizes us all. Hence the maxim: "Utmost happiness is when we do not strive for it, and highest praise consists in having no need for praise." (*Zhuangzi*)

◎孔子曰："请问游是。"老聃曰："夫得是，至美至乐也，得至美而游乎至乐，谓之至人。"（《庄子·田子方》）

（孔子说："请问游心于万物的本原状态是怎样的情景？"老聃说："达到这样的境界，就领略到极致的美，畅游于极致的快乐中，达到这种人生境界的人就称为'至人'。"）

Confucius asked: "When the heart roams free between heaven and earth, what will the scene look like?" Laozi answered: "Once a person has reached that realm, he will be able to savor beauty at its best and bask in extreme happiness. Such a person is known as a 'man of the highest order.'" (*Zhuangzi*)

主文而谲谏

／zhǔ wén ér jué jiàn／

Admonition Through Tactful Wording

诗歌在歌咏的同时以含蓄委婉的方式对执政者进行讽谏。“文”指有文采的歌咏；“谲”义为曲折变化，意思是不要直陈执政者的过失；“谏”就是规劝、谏诫。出自《毛诗序》。最初由儒家总结《诗经》的表达手法而提出，后来用为一切文艺作品应当遵循的标准。它的核心思想是，诗歌可以对执政者进行劝谏、讽刺，但要以含蓄委婉的言辞、比兴譬喻的方式寄托对执政者的批评以及对现实的不满。这一命题是儒家政治伦理在文学批评领域的具体表现。

This term shows that poetry should indirectly and mildly advise a ruler against wrongdoing. The critic should resort mainly to tactful and sensitive wording, trying not to appear blunt or offensive when admonishing the ruler. The term first appeared in the "Introductions to *Mao's Version of The Book of Songs*"; it was created by Confucian scholars in summarizing the various means of expression in *The Book of Songs*. Later, it became a criterion for measuring all works of art and literature. The core message is that, while poetry can be used to criticize or satirize a ruler and also to show discontent with social reality, a mild or indirect way should be employed, namely analogy, association, simile, and metaphor. This view is a manifestation of Confucian political ethics in the field of literary criticism.

引例 Citation:

◎上以风化下，下以风刺上。主文而谲谏，言之者无罪，闻之者足以戒，故曰风。（《毛诗序》）

（执政者用风诗教化百姓，百姓也用风诗讥刺执政者，用富于文采的诗歌对执政者含蓄委婉地进行劝讽，歌咏的人不会因此获罪，听闻诗歌的人足以引起警诫，所以将这类诗称作“风”。）

Rulers use *feng* (ballads) to cultivate the people and the people use them to ridicule the rulers. So long as a critic advises the monarch mildly and through beautiful poetry, he will not be found guilty and the monarch he criticizes will become more careful in making decisions. These poems are called *feng*. (Introductions to *Mao's Version of The Book of Songs*)

尊生

/zūnshēng/

Respect Life

尊重自己的生命，也尊重他人的生命。也说“重（zhòng）生”。生命属于每个人只有一次，任何人都不可轻易放弃生命，更不允许随意剥夺他人的生命。对于执政者而言，则要求以民众生命为重，尽可能满足民众正当的生存需求，不得做任何危害民众生命健康的事情。当然，不合道义的苟且偷生也是不被认可的。

This means respecting and valuing one's own life as well as that of others. Since each person has only one life to live, he does not easily give up his life and will not take away other people's lives. He who is in power should respect people's lives and do his utmost to uphold the people's legitimate right to life. He must not do anything harmful to people's life and health. On the other hand, he should not just allow his life to drift along without moral purpose.

引例 Citations:

◎“且吾闻之，不以所用养害所养。”……夫大（tài）王亶（dǎn）父可谓能尊生矣！能尊生者，虽贵富，不以养伤身；虽贫贱，不以利累形。（《庄子·让王》）

（“而且我听说，不能为了争夺养育人的东西而去伤害要养育的人。”……像太王亶父这样真可说是能尊重生命的了！能尊重生命的人，

即便富贵，也不会因为贪图享受而伤害身体；即便贫贱，也不会为了追求利禄而劳苦形体。）

“I have noticed that people often say that one must not hurt the nurtured in order to take the stuff used to nurture them.” ...People like Danfu, grandfather of King Wen of Zhou, truly respect life. He who respects life, though wealthy, does not harm his health because of enjoying luxury; he who respects life, though poor, does not exhaust his body in the seek of wealth and position. (*Zhuangzi*)

◎圣人深虑天下，莫贵于生。……天下，重物也，而不以害其生，又况于他物乎？惟不以天下害其生者也，可以托天下。（《吕氏春秋·贵生》）

（圣人深入思虑天下的事，认为没有什么东西比生命更宝贵。……天下是最重要的东西，可圣人不会因为它而危害自己的生命，又何况是其他东西呢？只有不会为了得到天下而危害自己生命的人，才可以把天下托付给他。）

The sage considered carefully about the things under heaven and thought that there was nothing more precious than life… State power was regarded as the most important, but the sage would not risk his life to secure it, let alone other things. State power should be entrusted to those who do not try to secure the power by endangering their own lives. (*Master Lü's Spring and Autumn Annals*)

◎故所谓尊生者，全生之谓；所谓全生者，六欲皆得其宜也。（《吕氏春秋·贵生》）

（所以，所谓尊重生命，说的就是保全生命；所谓保全生命，说的就是让人的各种基本欲望都能得到适当的满足。）

Therefore, what is meant by respecting life is preserving life, which, in turn, means satisfying people's justified desires. (*Master Lü's Spring and Autumn Annals*)

术语表

List of Concepts

英文	中文
A Country with Brave People Can Win the Victory.	民勇者战胜
A Dam of a Thousand Miles Can Collapse Due to an Ant Hole.	千里之堤，溃于蚁穴
A Good Ruler Does Not Cheat the People.	善为国者不欺其民
A Man of Virtue Seeks Dao, Not Livelihood.	君子谋道不谋食
A Master Physician to All the People	苍生大医
Admonition Through Tactful Wording	主文而谲谏
Advaya / Non-duality	不二
Apricot Trees / Venerable Doctors with Good Skills	杏林
Audience-based Education	因材施教
Banquet for Community Leaders and Rural Elders	乡饮酒礼
Be as Discreet at the End as at the Beginning; Remain Discreet Throughout the Whole Process	慎终如始

英文	中文
Bhūtatathatā / True Suchness	实相
Bold Expression of One's True Self	独抒性灵，不拘格套
Bronze Script	金文
Brothers and Sisters of the Same Parents; Compatriots	同胞
Buddhānusmṛti / Recollection of the Buddha	念佛
Cherish Life	好生
Cleverness and Clumsiness	巧拙
Concealment and Revelation	隐显
Consummate Interfusion	圆融
Criticism on *Ci* Poetry / *Cihua* (Story-telling with Song and Speech)	词话
Criticism on Poetry / *Shihua* (Story-telling with Song and Speech)	诗话
Denseness and Lightness	浓淡
Determine the Proper Way for Expressing Human Feelings	立中制节

英文	中文
Dharmakāya / Body of Dharma	法身
Disharmony / Harmony	隔 / 不隔
Dui (Marsh)	兑
Epigraph and Maxim	铭箴
Essay of Mourning and Essay of Memory	哀吊
Establish Moral Standards in Keeping with Human Feelings	称情立文
Eulogy or Inscription Carved on a Stela	诔碑
Even a Good Doctor Cannot Save a Doomed Patient.	良医不能救无命
Feeling Varies with Scenery and Verbal Expression Arises from Feeling.	情以物迁，辞以情发
Fighting Takes Courage.	夫战，勇气也
Form and Name	形名
Gen (Mountain)	艮
Great Healers Heal the Country.	上医医国

英文	中文
Great Physicians Treat Before the Outbreak of an Illness.	上工治未病
Hang a Gourd (Practice Medicine) to Help the World	悬壶济世
Harmony	和
Harmony Begets New Things.	和实生物
Hermit / Recluse	隐士
Human Heart / Human Desires	人心
Human Relations	人伦
Icchantika	一阐提
Ideas Cannot Match Actual Things and Words Cannot Fully Express Ideas.	意不称物，文不逮意
In War, Seek Quick Victory, Not Prolongation.	兵贵胜，不贵久
Inheritance and Innovation	因革
Inscriptions on Bones or Tortoise Shells	甲骨文
Keep a Low Profile	韬光养晦

英文	中文
Keep Earthly and Heavenly Affairs Separate	绝地天通
Lackluster Wording Never Travels Far.	言之无文，行而不远
Learn About What Is Forthcoming by Observing Tiny Clues	见微知著
Life Is as Important as Heaven.	人命关天
Listen to Both Sides	兼听
Love One's Own Kind	爱类
Make Writing Succinct	洗炼
Moral Mind / Moral Consciousness	道心
Much Blandishment and Little Criticism	劝百风一
Natural Attribute	分
Part Ways and Part Company	道不同，不相为谋
People's Grievances Harm the Country.	人怨伤国
Pinli (Diplomatic Etiquette and Protocol)	聘礼
Principle for the Application of Rules and Norms	絜矩之道

英文	中文
Public and Private	公私
Quiet Elegance	冲淡
Respect Life	尊生
Return Kindness with Kindness / Return Goodwill in Kind	投桃报李
Reversal to the Opposite	反
Rites of Archery	射礼
Satyadvaya / Two Truths	二谛
Self-treating an Illness Can Usually Get a Good Result.	有病不治，常得中医
Shame	耻
Sparsity and Density	疏密
Squareness and Roundness	方圆
Strength and Vigor	劲健
Take Precautions Early	防微杜渐
Tathāgatagarbha / Womb of the *Tathāgata*	如来藏

英文	中文
Teach by Example	身教
The Art of the Mind	心术
The Caring Heart of a Physician	医者仁心
The Jiangxi School of Poetry	江西诗派
The Jingling School of Literary Writing	竟陵派
The Key to Poetic Creation	诗家三昧
The Virtuous Love Mountains and the Wise Love Water.	仁者乐山，智者乐水
The Yuanhe Style of Poetry	元和体
There Is No Such Thing as Joyful or Sad Music.	声无哀乐
Thin and Strong	瘦硬
Those Adept at Coping with Defeat Cannot Be Destroyed.	善败者不亡
Those Who Most Love the People Will Eagerly Seek Talent.	爱人深者求贤急

英文	中文
Those Who Speak Shouldn't Be Punished While Those Who Listen Should Take Warning.	言者无罪，闻者足戒
To Delight in Life	乐生
To Impress Readers with True Feelings Oblivious of Its Wording	但见性情，不睹文字
Unadorned Antiquity	高古
Utmost Happiness Lies in Not Aware of the Happiness.	至乐无乐
Utter Innocence	赤子之心
Vijñāna / Consciousness	识
Virtuous Nature / Morals as Human Nature	德性
When Reaching an Extreme, Things Are Bound to Revert to Their Opposites.	物极必反
When the Birds Are Gone, the Bow Is Stored.	鸟尽弓藏

中国历史年代简表

A Brief Chronology of Chinese History

夏 Xia Dynasty		2070-1600 BC
商 Shang Dynasty		1600-1046 BC
周 Zhou Dynasty		1046-256 BC
周 Zhou Dynasty	西周 Western Zhou Dynasty	1046-771 BC
	东周 Eastern Zhou Dynasty	770-256 BC
秦 Qin Dynasty		221-206 BC
汉 Han Dynasty		206 BC-AD 220
汉 Han Dynasty	西汉 Western Han Dynasty	206 BC-AD 25
	东汉 Eastern Han Dynasty	25-220
三国 Three Kingdoms		220-280
三国 Three Kingdoms	魏 Kingdom of Wei	220-265
	蜀 Kingdom of Shu	221-263
	吴 Kingdom of Wu	222-280
晋 Jin Dynasty		265-420
晋 Jin Dynasty	西晋 Western Jin Dynasty	265-317
	东晋 Eastern Jin Dynasty	317-420

<table>
<tr><td colspan="3">南北朝 Southern and Northern Dynasties</td><td>420-589</td></tr>
<tr><td rowspan="12">南北朝
Southern
and
Northern
Dynasties</td><td colspan="2">南朝 Southern Dynasties</td><td>420-589</td></tr>
<tr><td rowspan="4">南朝
Southern
Dynasties</td><td>宋 Song Dynasty</td><td>420-479</td></tr>
<tr><td>齐 Qi Dynasty</td><td>479-502</td></tr>
<tr><td>梁 Liang Dynasty</td><td>502-557</td></tr>
<tr><td>陈 Chen Dynasty</td><td>557-589</td></tr>
<tr><td colspan="2">北朝 Northern Dynasties</td><td>386-581</td></tr>
<tr><td rowspan="5">北朝
Northern
Dynasties</td><td>北魏 Northern Wei Dynasty</td><td>386-534</td></tr>
<tr><td>东魏 Eastern Wei Dynasty</td><td>534-550</td></tr>
<tr><td>北齐 Northern Qi Dynasty</td><td>550-577</td></tr>
<tr><td>西魏 Western Wei Dynasty</td><td>535-556</td></tr>
<tr><td>北周 Northern Zhou Dynasty</td><td>557-581</td></tr>
<tr><td colspan="3">隋 Sui Dynasty</td><td>581-618</td></tr>
<tr><td colspan="3">唐 Tang Dynasty</td><td>618-907</td></tr>
</table>

五代 Five Dynasties		907-960
五代 Five Dynasties	后梁 Later Liang Dynasty	907-923
	后唐 Later Tang Dynasty	923-936
	后晋 Later Jin Dynasty	936-947
	后汉 Later Han Dynasty	947-950
	后周 Later Zhou Dynasty	951-960
宋 Song Dynasty		960-1279
宋 Song Dynasty	北宋 Northern Song Dynasty	960-1127
	南宋 Southern Song Dynasty	1127-1279
辽 Liao Dynasty		907-1125
金 Jin Dynasty		1115-1234
元 Yuan Dynasty		1206-1368
明 Ming Dynasty		1368-1644
清 Qing Dynasty		1616-1911
中华民国 Republic of China		1912-1949
中华人民共和国 People's Republic of China		Founded on October 1, 1949